THE FOUR GOSPELS

PATRICK FANNON, S.M.M.

THE
FOUR
GOSPELS

A

Short Introduction to
Their Making and Message

FIDES PUBLISHERS, INC.

NOTRE DAME, INDIANA

CONTENTS

Für
Leni, Hildegarde und Lorle Schäffler

FOREWORD

This short introduction to the making and the message of the Gospels comprises six articles which appeared in *Scripture* (the first two chapters of the present book) and in the *Clergy Review* (the remaining four chapters). They have been somewhat pruned to avoid unnecessary repetition, and subtitles have been added. I am grateful to the editors of both reviews for their kind permission for the articles to appear in their present form.

PATRICK FANNON, S.M.M.
Church Stretton.

THE FORMATION OF THE GOSPELS

CONTEMPORARY biblical scholarship has achieved surprising results in many fields of its large acreage, and one of its most rewarding successes has been to trace the growth of the Gospels, isolating in their development the various graftings and cross-fertilizations which finally produced such a prodigious plant. No longer are the Gospels viewed as having sprung up mushroom-like overnight. A relatively long and complicated process has been discerned before the prize fruit emerged.

It is in an attempt to trace in broad outline this process that this chapter is offered; not, presumptuously, to those who patiently labour in such fields, but to those, as it were, at the marketing end—who take their Scripture from the scripturists. For purposes of convenience rather than of necessity, the growth of the Gospels will be considered as following five stages (though the unwary should be warned that such clear docketing sacrifices something of the elusive interplay of factors which made for the formation of the Gospels). In the first place we are faced

with the primitive preaching (or *kerygma*) which
was the seed containing the traits later development would manifest. Then there is the first
development in and through tradition, in the
transmitting of the Christian message. This was
followed by attempts at committing to writing
that primitive message, and these attempts, in
their turn, led to the actual formation of the
Gospels. Finally, certain "finishing touches"
must be considered.

It must be stated emphatically that the enquiry
into the formation of the Gospels is nowhere
near complete. Much still remains to be done—
the sifting of material, the re-examination of
theories, the elaboration and consolidation of
stable gains. Yet the outline of this fascinating
growth has been observed, and a new approach
to the content of the Gospels is hardening into
what must become an entrenched method.

The primitive preaching

The prime efforts of the Apostles to extend
Christ's message of salvation were by preaching;
writing was not their first preoccupation. Like
Christ himself, they proclaimed the "Good
News". And this apostolic message is best
expressed by what the New Testament calls the
kerygma (1 Cor. 1.21)—the content of that early

missionary preaching to win to the Faith those not yet of it. In that dawn of the New Dispensation the spoken word was the warhead of the Christian conquest. In its pulsing immediacy the Apostles limited themselves to essentials, reserving to the *didache* (teaching) the more complete formation of their converts. Hence it is that the *kerygma* appears in the New Testament as *the* fundamental message, as the basis presupposed by all the later reflections of which it would become the object and by the diverse theologies which Paul, John and the author of Hebrews would construct on it.

We have now to enquire whether it be possible to isolate the actual content of that message.

There are two principal sources for studying the apostolic preaching: the Pauline epistles and the primitive discourses of the Acts of the Apostles. The early speeches of Peter in Acts (2.22–4,32–3;3.12–26; and particularly 10.36–43, which is like a ground-plan of the Synoptic Gospels) betray, by the archaism of their theology and their numerous Semitisms, that they come from written and oral sources of very ancient and often Palestinian origin. Further, their schematic character and the type of phrases occurring indicate their genesis from formularies of the primitive preaching, which formularies

were a natural consequence of a message that had
to be repeated time and time again.

Comparing the Pauline *kerygma* and that of
the discourses in Acts, we can characterize the
fundamental message of the Apostles as that of
the passion and resurrection of Christ proclaimed
as the inauguration of the era when the divine
promises are realized. The latter days have
arrived, even if only inceptively; the Messiah
and Saviour of Israel is now enthroned; men
must repent and turn to God. A frequent recourse to the ancient Scriptures is noticeable, not
so much to demonstrate, after the manner of
apologetics, the truth of the affirmations being
made about Christ, as to situate these in the full
stream of revelation and of the long history of
salvation as the present fulfilment of God's long-
awaited design.

In this proclamation the earthly ministry of
Christ must be referred to, not only to introduce
the One about whom the Resurrection is
affirmed, but because in that ministry are already
manifested the signs of the intervention of God
bringing in the era of salvation. Hence are mentioned also the Davidic descent of Christ and the
miracles by which God accredited him. In this
perspective the events of the ministry are not
separated from the Passion and Resurrection,
but with them enter into a context which clari-

fies their absolute and definitive value as salvific events.

And so before the Christ-Event was committed to writing, there was a period of preaching which was later to have a formative influence on the written Gospels. In the Synoptic Gospels we shall find broadening out into an arterial road of doctrine the tiny trail of theology only traced in the Acts of the Apostles. The preaching of John the Baptist, the baptism of Christ, the beginning of the Galilean ministry, healings and exorcisms, the ministry in Jerusalem, the Crucifixion and Resurrection—this outline served as a framework into which anecdotes of Christ's mission, power, teaching, by some incident or memorable saying, parable etc., could be inserted.

But it should be noted that these accounts of incidents of Christ's life and his sayings were used by preachers to illustrate their teaching on Christ before they came to be written up in the Gospels. Attempts, with varying success, have been made to classify these "units". Perhaps a broad classification only would be permitted by our present state of knowledge. There are first of all the *sayings* of Christ which are enveloped in a description of an incident—a miracle, a controversy or an episode of the life of Christ. Here, the main point to be made is in the saying, and everything else is subordinate and directed

to that saying. If the incident is a miracle, it is
hardly described; the saying is the important
thing. A good example of this is in the account
of the healing of the man with the withered
hand. (Mark 3.1–5.) The emphasis is not on the
miracle but on Christ's saying, "Is it lawful on
the sabbath to do good or to do harm, to save
life or to kill?" Also in Christ's controversies;
the dialogue is brief, incisive, destined to place
in relief a saying of Christ (cf. Matt. 22.15–22 on
the tribute to Caesar). Even when the saying is
embodied in a description of an incident in the
life of Christ, the same sobriety in the description is once more noticeable in order to under-
line the saying (cf. Matt. 19.13–15, on Christ
blessing the children). In accounts which deal
specifically with the value of Christ's *miracles*,
we find that here everything is directed towards
emphasizing the miracle. These accounts are
constructed after a regular fashion: circumstances of the miracle, the miracle itself, the
effect produced. Details abound to place in relief,
not the saying, but the action of Christ. Then
there are accounts primarily destined to sketch
the *person* of Christ (e.g., Matt. 15.21–5, the
incident of the Canaanite woman, which served
to portray Christ *vis-à-vis* the pagans). Finally,
there are *summaries* and *transitions* which re-
sume the activity of Christ either in words or

miracles (e.g., the account of Christ at Nazareth, Luke 4.16–30, where Luke seems to have combined three visits to form one inaugural scene on Christ's mission of grace and its refusal by his own people).

All these accounts, which are constructed with wonderful economy, bear the marks of popular preaching and tradition in which a much-repeated story is rubbed down and polished until nothing but the hard core remains in its most arresting form. The "evangelists" (charismatic preachers, cf. Acts 21.8; Eph. 4.11; 2 Tim. 4.5) recounted, in their early preaching, those "evangelical" memoirs under a form which tended to become fixed by repetition—and our Gospels in their small units are tributary to this influence.

And so the irreducible minimum of the apostolic message with its crystallized accounts of incidents from Christ's life was to provide the constants of our Gospels, not only as regards matter, but particularly as regards doctrinal emphasis.

Development in transmission

But in the very transmission of the Christian message, the fundamental *credo* was adapted to the circumstances of the hearers. Peter, speaking to Palestinians, underlines the messianicity of Jesus; Paul, on the Gentile mission, shows Jesus as the Saviour whose work has a universal character; John, addressing persons of a more mature Christianity, was able to show the value lying beneath the events of the life of Christ.

On the rebound, the primitive Christian communities had their questions to ask on problems which arose from day-to-day preoccupations: marriage, divorce, widowhood, Jewish ritual, Jewish laws, categories of people ("publicans", sinners, non-Israelites). These, and a host of other considerations, were influential in effecting, not only a choice of incidents from Christ's life and ministry which answered new situations in the Church, but also an interpretation of them in the light of contemporary problems. It has been thanks to recent researches that the Gospel units—narratives, sayings, parables etc.,—have been plunged into the great stream of faith and life of the primitive Church. Some success has been achieved in segregating various formative influences from the primitive community in the production of our Gospels: preaching, apologetics, doctrine, liturgy.

The result of this intervention of the community in the formation of tradition has an important corollary: there was a certain elaboration, or better, a penetration of all Christ did and said so that the multiform riches of that Event could be of value to the Church. Hence, it must be clearly understood that the facts and sayings so reported are not, in each individual case, to be taken as a rigorously exact reproduction of what actually happened. Note how the same event or saying is transmitted differently in many cases by the different Evangelists. Further, the inevitable laws of all human testimony and of its transmission dissuade from demanding such material exactitude. In the course of transmission, many of the Gospel facts and sayings lost their original link with time and place, and it would often be a mistake to take seriously such connections as "on that day", "then", "afterwards".

But these remarks in no way prejudice the validity of the facts that were transmitted. The Church did not create facts; she interpreted them. And the Holy Ghost sponsored the whole programme of the Church—tradition as well as inspiration. He guided the work of elaboration, guaranteeing for the results that true inerrancy which is not so much concerned with brute facts as with the spiritual message enshrined in them.

Written accounts begin

As the first eyewitnesses began to pass away, an attempt was made to fix the traditions by writing. The previously isolated incidents tended to be grouped together, often after a chronological fashion—as Mark 1.16–39, which presents a rounded picture of a day at Capharnaum—or in a systematic way, as in the five great sections of Matthew where related subject-matter is given together. From being small sections at the beginning, these groupings later developed into larger collections.

It seems more than likely that the very early written attempts formed small vade-mecums which could easily have served the preachers and catechists in their missionary work. The authors of these collections, tiny instalments of the Gospel, are unknown to us and nothing remains of their work except what has been incorporated into the canonical Gospels which supplanted them.

But between these collections and our Gospels there is still another factor to be considered: editions of Gospel material—"gospels" in lower case, we might call them—which were the approximate preparation for our present Gospels. As far as can be ascertained by present studies, it would seem that this process reached a climax in two great series of edited material: one would be a Galilean-ministry source and the other the Passion narrative which, though embracing more than the account of the Passion itself, would nevertheless have this as its centre of reference.

Our Gospels appear

With the very writing of the Gospels after this period of editings, we come up against the thorny problem of the interrelationship of Matthew, Mark and Luke—the Synoptic Problem. A treatment of this vexatious and apparently insoluble problem is outside our scope, but it has a relevancy in so far as it touches on the formation of our Gospels. Before canonical Matthew, Mark and Luke were written, was there a "Matthean" source comprising a Greek translation of Aramaic Matthew plus supplementary material which was pressed into service for our canonical Gospels? Or did a Greek translation of Aramaic Matthew lie at the basis of just Matthew and Luke, who were both dependent also on Mark? No definite solution has yet been proposed. Certainly Matthew and Luke owe something to a common written source and to Mark.

But they did not hesitate to change a source or sources common to them. The Evangelists were no mere compilers. And once more we are in the presence of another factor in the Gospel formation: intentional changes. These, like the inevitable accidents of transmission referred to above, may also give rise to differences of testimony. In many cases the editors of the Gospel consciously wished to present things in a different fashion. Before them oral tradition, whose heirs they were, had not scrupled to interpret and adapt in different ways to suit the needs of the living Faith the matter under transmission.

A comparison among the Synoptists provides interesting examples of this tendency at work. Matthew and Mark, in their accounts of the trial and crucifixion, portray the Jews and Pilate as definitely hostile to Christ; John and Luke, on the contrary, present a crowd which is more curious than hostile, and Pilate's scourging of Jesus is more by way of precluding further demands of the Jews—death—than by way of punishment. The interpretations given to some of the parables vary considerably—e.g., in that of the Sower. Luke, writing his Gospel at a time when the Church was free from persecution, shows Christ as exhorting Christians to bring forth fruit in patience amid the trials of everyday life. (Luke 8.11–15.) The other two Synoptists have a different situation in mind—a time of tribulation (Mark 4.14–20) and of persecution (Matt. 13.18–23). These and a number of other points show a certain plasticity in the handling of some details of tradition by the Evangelists.

Once more it must be recalled that just as the Evangelists received matter already elaborated by tradition in view of situations in the Church under the influence of the *magisterium*, that coefficient of the action of the Holy Ghost, so too under the same influence they were empowered to sound the depth of Christ's message and apply their discoveries to all available fields of Christian existence. The message of salvation was held to no law of diminishing returns. Further, if the Holy Ghost has not seen fit to demand from his interpreters perfect uniformity in detail, it is because he does not lay importance for the Faith on material precision. We can even say that he has wanted this difference in testimony—a fact so attested by diverse and discordant traditions (e.g., the accounts of the post-Resurrection narratives) assumes deep within itself a rich dimension of truth. The Evangelists cannot be accused of having falsified with tendentious motives the facts of the Christian message; rather, those facts had found four conscientious interpreters whose efforts were accompanied and accredited by an untiring Spirit of God.

This being understood, the Gospels must be seen primarily as works of doctrine rather than as biographies. It must be understood, too, that a gospel itself is a literary form laid under contribution to proclaim the message of salvation. A gospel is not essentially a history. It is the announcement of salvation wrought by Christ. With matter which they certainly held as historical, the sacred authors have made a work

whose centre of interest is not strictly the writing
of history *ut sic*. A gospel is really the apostolic
preaching, a restatement of the *kerygma* in valid
historical terms. It is history certainly, but history which is clarified in the light of events; in
fact, history read backwards, theologically interpreted and applied to circumstances. But this
theological interpretation is not perversion. It
serves to heighten implications of Christ's coming which might too easily have been lost in a
mere restatement of colourless records. This was
a major consideration throughout the formation
of the Gospels.

Stop-press additions

But even when the Gospels were formed and,
as it were, began to enjoy the dignity of capitals,
the last word had not yet been said; there were
stop-press additions: a point of belief to be
explained or developed, a finishing touch to be
made. Hence it is that the Infancy Narratives in
Matthew and Luke, representing a maturer reflection of the primitive Church which sought
to go back to the very beginning of the Christ
story, were added. Mark 16.9–20 were added to
the Gospel whose lack of conclusion was as
obvious as a missing tooth—a fact which an inspired author corrected.

A word finally on the Fourth Gospel. This

differs greatly from the earlier three and rarely runs parallel to them. It has a problem all its own. Appearing long after the Synoptics, it represents a more advanced stage in theological reflection. But if its elaboration has been slow and gradual, still it contains very ancient elements which may well enshrine the primitive preaching of John.

Any study of the formation of the Gospels must floodlight the importance of the Church's tradition in interpreting the events of Christ's life. Faith is a living thing; but its life can only be sustained in and by the Church. And her office it was, under the guiding finger of the Holy Spirit, to penetrate the mystery of Christ. There was no call for her to "create" events—she had sufficient matter on which to ruminate. The term of her primitive reflections, which were stimulated by her everyday life of faith, is presented to us in our Gospels, in those "Minutes", if you wish, which summarize the meeting of God and man.

2

CAN WE KNOW JESUS?

THOSE who have been accustomed to read their Gospels as primarily an account of the life of our Lord, or those who, over a number of years, have used for their spiritual reading and instruction those "Lives of Jesus" which have long since established themselves as family favourites, will be prepared to answer this question with a vigorous affirmative. Surely, you will hear them saying, we are able to follow in great detail all the events of Christ's life from the Crib to the Cross, all he did and said—we even know the where and when of it all. Others, who, perhaps in the course of a secondary education or on a higher level, have cut their biblical teeth on Scripture textbooks and have been introduced to such perennial difficulties as the Synoptic Problem or the relation of John to the Synoptists, have become aware that the writers of our Gospels do not always agree in their accounts and have to be "harmonized". And when this procedure—stretched to the breaking-point of an already remarkable elasticity—has refused to surrender a solution—e.g., of why Matthew re-

counted a saying of Christ in circumstances differing from those containing the same saying in
Luke—the long arm of coincidence has indicated
an exit from the problem: the saying, the event,
happened twice.

The problem

But more enquiring minds have not always
been convinced of this approach to the question
of the life of our Lord; it has appeared *simpliste*.
We have seen in the last chapter that the recent
investigation into the formation of the Gospels
shows how their growth was dependent on various
factors: preaching, which limited itself to providing essential data about Christ; the tradition
of the Church, which transmitted that message
within the living framework of its life and faith;
lastly, the work of the Evangelists as the climax
of that process which resulted in our Gospels as
the written record of redemption. And because
they were precisely that, they were not, in the
first place, a history but a theology, the sacred
writers being dedicated more to the significance
of what Christ said and did than to merely cata-
loguing the incidents of a crowded life. A certain
unconcern is noticeable in matters of chronology
and geography, and there is not always agree-
ment as to the exact words used by Christ. But
these points, and many others, were secondary to

writers whose main intention was to offer their readers the meaning of Christ's life and teaching.

Yet such a view of the Gospels as theology rather than history (even though this latter is not excluded) raises an important question, or rather a series of questions. If the Gospels are primarily designed to teach Christ's message, so much so that the facts of his life have only a lesser importance, and if that message is presented to us as it was understood by the primitive Church, how can we know Jesus as he was? Further, if we cannot know Jesus as he was, is there not a danger that ignorance will father denial—not only of Jesus but even of his doctrine? Now, this is not a new problem, and there is something to be learned by tracing briefly its origin and development before attempting to discuss the historical value of the Gospel witness and the question as to whether a biography of Christ is possible.

David Strauss and the Jesus of history

In the heyday of nineteenth-century liberal Protestantism, the notion took shape that the historical person of Jesus—who was born in Bethlehem, walked the streets of Nazareth, journeyed through the Judean hills to Jerusalem, there to suffer and be sentenced to death—was a much lowlier figure than he around whom our beliefs are centred. This smaller figure, it was claimed, had received a new and completely idealistic stature—that of the Christ of faith, a product of myth fashioned to accommodate the over-credulous. D. F. Strauss contested the belief that the Christ of faith was the Jesus of history— a pernicious distinction which soon hardened into a separation. And with it, the axe was laid to the root: henceforth, one of the basic problems of Christology was how our belief in Christ was to be historically defended and explained.

Strauss was followed by a galaxy of liberal and rationalist scholars who, in their different ways, applied his principle to their researches on our Lord, and the result was a spate of "Lives of Jesus" which bypassed any possible supernatural associations with the Christ of faith, and concentrated on the purely human characteristics of our Lord. And so we have, for example, Renan's classic picture which turned Jesus into the ideal of a humanitarian religion, after casting aside the "suspect" theology of the New Testament because it was "unhistorical". Even today, when that "Jesus of history" movement has passed away, we can still discern faint traces of it in an emphasis on the humanity of Christ —which may well offer the required corrective to many of the ultra-radical modern views we have now to examine.

Rudolf Bultmann and the Christ of faith

The rise of form criticism (which investigated the various units making up our Gospels for their place in the primitive Church) after the First World War signalled a new and contrasting line of studies around the subject of Christ. No longer was the historical Palestinian Jesus the subject of enquiry in the shape of "critical" biographies, but rather, the previously rejected Christ of faith was invited back to dominate the discussions. Whereas before an absorbing interest was shown in the details of his earthly life, now, it was affirmed, these are of no significance and indeed cannot be known in isolation. Independent criticism had really boxed the compass—but its latest voyage was to end in failure, even if some soundings were made which would serve to plot the true course to an appreciation of Christ.

Rudolf Bultmann has loomed large on the contemporary scene in the new criticism and has not hesitated to push to their logical conclusions directives offered by some earlier critics. On the question of the historicity of Christ, Bultmann's thesis may be thus briefly resumed: There is not in the Gospels any account or saying of Christ which does not primarily reflect the faith of the Church; what we know is not Christ but the faith of the primitive community *about* him. This extreme position of affirming that Christ cannot be known independently of the representations made by the faith of his disciples (already suggested by Wellhausen) is due to Bultmann's philosophy, which separates history from faith, and also to his sociological theories, which attribute to the human mass a true creative power. This historical scepticism about our ability to know the Gospel figure of Christ is joined in Bultmann to the conviction that the New Testament must be "demythologised", that is, freed from the shackles of a primitive thought-form and re-expressed in a form intelligible to the twentieth-century mind. But that is not all. He has gone on to interpret Christ in terms of existential philosophy, to signify not so much a person in time and space as an announcement that God comes to man.

Against such views there has been, in the last decade, a noteworthy reaction. It has been well observed that Continental opinions are watered down when they cross the Channel, and this school of thought never boasted an English department. But it is perhaps the recent Scandinavian scholars who have most strikingly rejected such proposals. In an address delivered at the opening session of the Oxford Congress on "The Four Gospels in 1957", Harald Riesenfeld, Professor at the University of Uppsala, stressed a decided return to a more traditional view: the

Gospel tradition should be traced to Jesus himself, and not to the primitive Church. And among Bultmann's disciples there has been a marked change of climate, even if a certain historical scepticism still survives among them, the tattered remains of the master's mantle. Among Catholics, his theories on Christ received no sympathetic recognition, but it was not till the last few years that a worthwhile attempt was made to attack his position radically.

Revelation of Christ tied to history

Such, in outline, are the main trends of discussion about the historical Christ which emanated from non-Catholic scholars, and they will be seen to be related to two centres of reference, the Jesus of history and the Christ of faith, which postulate an invalid separation between history and faith. Before we can hope to present a solution to the problem of Christ, that gap must be closed.

Revelation, we are becoming increasingly aware, was given not only in history but intimately tied to the events of a particular people's history, that of the Jews. The raw material which revelation made use of was the everyday life of a definite race-group, its members, their lives and loves, joys and sorrows, their homes in the fertile countryside of Galilee or amidst the rugged splendour of the hills of Judah. Salvation was to come to us wrapped in a Jewish covering. And the whole perspective of the New Testament is this salvation within history: God was revealing himself *in history*. The faith that was required of the primitive Church was a faith which was based on historical facts, as the missionary preaching recorded in the Acts of the Apostles testifies. Without such a starting-point, the message preached would be meaningless. Hence, in the primitive tradition, faith and history are indissolubly linked, and to the New Testament authors not only is their history factual, but they clearly consider that their faith is true only in so far as it corresponds with the truth of the facts reported. For them faith was not to be reduced to an act of total abandonment without any human guarantee, since fideism or faith alone would pave the way to unbelief. Faith must include an object, a fact—namely, a return in some way or other to history. There is no radical opposition between the order of positive scientific knowledge and the order of faith, and in the New Testament we are dealing not only with preached doctrine but also with historical data. Faith was based on fact.

And the faith of the primitive Church was based on the historical fact of the life and teaching of Jesus Christ. The significance of Jesus, his person, his work and the events of his life only appear with the place he occupies in the history of salvation; God was revealing himself in Christ. Even if we acknowledge that the growth of the Gospels knew multiple stages and that their elements underwent transforming influences in the primitive Church according as a living faith interpreted them and sounded their depths, it is still possible to reach a sure knowledge of the facts, sayings, life and person of Jesus. And this because once the layers of tradition are defined, we must perceive an irreducible substratum; the unanimous affirmation of the sources and of a witness which attaches faith to concrete facts and real sayings, in a known period and in a known place. It is clear, moreover, that the Gospel writers' will to consign to paper the work of salvation by Jesus Christ, a theological preoccupation, corresponded with the intention to offer a true history.

Testimony and history

Now in the mind of the primitive Church, Christ was not a person of the past but the risen Lord, present with his will and power, the one who now offered salvation. The formulas of its preaching in relating his history declare that he *is* and not that he was. What has taken place is understood according to its significance for today, and this today is no calendar date but the present such as God has made it, opening out into the future according to his design. The earthly revelation of Jesus is still an actual revelation and in this perspective his words are dressed with the concerns of the Church.

Hence the development of a tradition informed by faith is not a product of the imagination, not a creation of the mass, but the response to the mission of Jesus considered as a whole, the affirmation of a situation proper to him whose life began in Galilee to finish on the Cross, and who now reveals himself as Lord. And so tradition, in each of its stages, witnesses the reality of his history and of his resurrection.

And so testimony which was designed to arouse faith could not be a simple, material repetition of the deeds and sayings of Christ, the vehicle of revelation for all time. Indeed, any historical study worthy of the name will include more than a list of events—it is only in those small *aides-mémoires* which prepare the eleventh-hour student for the coming ordeal that such a procedure is adopted. No, events must be considered according to their significance and the Evangelists, who were supremely qualified to do this, have not hesitated to interpret for us the life of Christ. Moreover, to reflect on the significance of an event is already one way of affirming that fact. The result is, of course, that theology and history have been interwoven, perhaps inextricably, and while it is necessary to search for history in the *kerygma*, it is also necessary to discover the *kerygma* in history.

We may rightly reject the tempting simplification of the Jesus-of-history school, which would concentrate on describing the merely human traits of our Lord, isolated from all contact with his divine mission. Equally we may reject the Christ-of-faith approach, which, ignoring any human factors, would examine purely theological considerations. The Church of the incarnate Word has always taken her stand between the extremes of Arianism and Docetism, whatever the guises their latter-day progeny may don. And this is really the key to the problem; the human and the divine are both present in Christ and both lurk behind the Church's written testimony to him. In it both find a place, and we must resolutely decline to accept any pattern of investigation which would sacrifice one in favour of the other. There is a harmony here, and even if it has been the Church's first care to teach us this accord, she has not neglected to tell us that the notes which compose it are very real.

Consequently the assertions of those critics who write off the Gospel accounts of Christ and his doctrine as the unwarranted creation of the primitive community cannot be sustained, for the simple reason that the Church did not need to create; she had sufficient matter to exploit. That this exploitation took the form of adaptation, actualization, answers to questions posed by the nascent Church, redactional procedures in which a diversity of milieux, objects and forms played an influential role cannot be denied. That she allowed incidental differences of chronology, geography and even emphasis in reporting the words of Christ is also evident, as a comparison of the four Gospels will show. Yet, once more, exploitation is not creation but the attempt to excavate the hidden riches that lie buried in Christ and in his message. The Church did not need to salt her mine.

Admittedly, it would be difficult for us to try to disengage from their theological context all the facts and sayings of Christ's life, to take the Christology out of Christ, so to speak. But, as has been suggested above, this may well prove a false problem. Separate those events from their meaningful presentation and they become meaningless. If scholars are directing research towards discovering the most primitive strata of the Gospel accounts, they are principally concerned to trace the development in tradition of the Christian message. They cannot hope to unearth new and unexpected details of the life of Christ.

The portrait which the Gospels sketch for us of
Christ is sufficiently clear to establish in our
minds his person and his mission. We may not
always be sure of the time or place of an incident,
not always informed of the *ipsissima verba* he
pronounced on a number of occasions. But the
important thing, the thing that really matters,
is the content of what he did and said; and this
is ours. We know him as he was.

No biography but a memoir

Are we able, then, to have a biography of
Jesus? It has been indicated earlier in this chapter how this question would seem to have been
answered by the numerous "Lives of Jesus"
which have an honoured place on our library
shelves. It is not as simple as that, however. We
have seen how the Evangelists were first and
foremost concerned to transmit the doctrinal
significance of Christ's life. His story was of
secondary importance, even if the facts recounted
have their value as providing material for a
knowledge of Christ, as well as offering sources
for that doctrine.

A useful distinction must be made when we
speak of a "Life of Jesus". Let us say straight
away that the ideal sought after in the last century of a critical *biography* in a strict sense,
namely a presentation of Christ which traces in

some detail his development, both psychological and in his relations with external circumstances, is not feasible. Not only do we lack the mass of information such a biography would require. The Evangelists have not been over-generous in furnishing such data, nor, given their aim, could they be expected to do so. Even such an obvious requirement as an adequate chronology is lacking: scholars cannot agree whether Christ's public ministry lasted one, two or three years. Given this situation, we can understand how a Scripture scholar of such learning as Fr Lagrange was led to renounce his intention of writing a life of Jesus according to the classical formula.

What, however, can and must be our ideal is undoubtedly a memoir of Jesus—the collection of facts that we have about him, some chain of events, some links of cause and effect in these events. And this is possible. We have a significant and decisive minimum of facts; there is a general curve in their incidence from Galilee to Jerusalem; and there is an explanation of that graph. It must be admitted that numerous details, and often important ones to our way of thinking, escape us, but, as we have already remarked, the Gospels offer us such an impact with the personality enshrined in their pages as to make good the deficiencies which a strict historical method would deplore. Needless to say, such an historical portrait of Christ, were it to prescind from the supernatural dimension of Christ's character, would be no more than a travesty of his true likeness and would offer nothing more than a pale reflection of his reality.

In conclusion, we may state that our Gospels present us with sufficient reliable matter to give us an appreciation of Christ as he was, since their witness is anchored in history. The Christ of faith is no fascinating by-product of the Church nor a lengthened silhouette of the humble figure of Jesus of Nazareth. The Jesus of history and the Christ of faith are one person, Jesus Christ, and this cornerstone of our faith is no prefabrication. We do not know all we should wish to know about him, led perhaps by an idle curiosity; but the Evangelists have seen to it that we know all that is necessary. His "Lives" may often try to establish conditions of time and place for incidents which the Evangelists were content simply to join to a previous memory; they may try also to smooth down with the heavy plane of "harmonization" the knotty problems of discrepancy and the hard edges of discordance. In a word, they may try to offer us the satisfying continuity of a well-planned biography with the details of a diary. But this is a hope which exceeds its promise, and the promise of the Gospels was to tell us of salvation and of how Christ by his life and death and resurrection wrought it. Here was not just another life to be written, but a life to be preached.

3

ST MARK'S MESSAGE

Modern interest in Mark

IF we could recall to earth some scholar who had lived in the centuries which followed the first preaching of the Gospel there is a balance of possibilities in favour of his being overwhelmed by the modern interest in the Gospel according to St Mark. The Early Church, whose descriptions of this Evangelist include what we may term the sublime ("divine abbreviator" of the Gospels) and the near-ridiculous ("stump-fingered"), shows little sign of the current preoccupation with the Second Gospel. The fact was that St Matthew, with his detailed accounts of Christ's teaching, held the field. But if you wanted a brief, eminently readable report on the events of Christ's life, or if (like St Jerome) you wanted to give your monks some worthwhile, non-Italianate spiritual reading—there was Mark. In the armoury of Sacred Scripture, St Mark was small-arms.

We should have to explain to our *revenant* that St Mark owes his unexpected favour in great part to three centres of discussion on the origin and nature of the Gospels during the last century. In the first place, there was (as we saw in the last chapter) the "Jesus-of-history" movement, which contrived to separate the humble figure of Jesus of Nazareth from the teaching surrounding him in the New-Testament accounts. A Gospel which appeared to offer a minimum account of doctrine would seem to have interfered less with the historical Jesus. Hence, the factual, down-to-earth Gospel of Mark was an obvious choice for those who wanted the story of Jesus without the trimmings. He lacked St Matthew's long Sermon on the Mount, his long Chapter 13 giving the parables, his apologetics, his Church organization. The unvarnished historical truth in Mark, the liberal theologians claimed, made him the primitive Gospel, a sort of evangelical *ombudsman*, reference to whom would settle all disputes as to the life of Jesus of Nazareth.

However, at the beginning of this century, a new note could be detected in the echoes coming from the hammer of higher criticism. Wilhelm Wrede, in 1903, proposed the thesis that Mark was just as theological as Matthew, Luke and John (a remarkable bouquet for Mark—even if it was intended as a brickbat). He, no less than they, was concerned to present a Christ of faith and (like them) lost for us the historical Jesus under a mass of doctrine. Mark, consequently, was equally unreliable. Wrede's suggestion was quickly taken up by other critics and a hurried expedition was organized to discover what were Mark's sources; surely there, it was hoped, the original, uncontaminated evidence for the Jesus of history must be hidden. But a tocsin was soon to sound for the "Jesus-of-history" movement. In 1906 Albert Schweitzer's *The Quest of the Historical Jesus* (its later English title) was published and it signalled the end to the long enterprise of liberal "lives of Jesus" and of the liberal reading of Christianity which was erected on them. Schweitzer, whatever his other faults, emphasized that there was a deeper dimension to Christ than that of milk-and-water humanitarianism; there was the dimension of the eternal.

The second centre of discussion which gave the Marcan account its latter-day significance was the enquiry into the relationship of the Gospels of Matthew, Mark and Luke to one another— the Synoptic Problem. The traditional view that Matthew was the first Gospel (written in Aramaic and later translated into Greek) and that Mark and Luke followed him and were dependent on him came under heavy fire. Various theories were proposed, extended, qualified, but in practically all of them non-Catholic

scholars remained convinced of one thing: of our
four Gospels, Mark was first. Not only that; he
supplied a framework for Matthew and Luke.
If it is possible to summarize the present position, we may say that for one group of scholars
(Germans and English, mostly) Matthew and
Luke are dependent for their sources on Mark,
on a common fund of what is principally matter
composed of sayings and discourses of Christ
(called "Q" or, as Fr Wikenhauser terms it, a
Greek translation of Matthew's small Aramaic
Gospel), and (in the case of Luke, anyway) on
unknown sources. Another group of scholars,
led by the Catholics Vaganay, Cerfaux and
Benoit, place, at the source of the text we now
possess of all three Synoptists, common material
in the form of a Greek translation of Aramaic
Matthew plus supplementary material. However,
for the majority of New-Testament scholars,
Catholic and non-Catholic, Mark would be the
first of our Gospels in their present canonical
form.

Finally, the third development in modern
studies in which Mark received further attention
was the investigation of that oral tradition which
took literary shape in the Gospels. The stories
and sayings recorded in these previously circu-
lated, we saw in Chapter 1, by word of mouth
in the numerous Christian communities through

their preachers. This school of thought will try to define the patterns or forms which these oral traditions received and even the reasons which contributed to their preservation. An effort is made, then, to take us behind the scenes of our written Gospels and observe the primitive Church *en famille*. We might recall here that the Gospels were the climax of a process which included preaching, early attempts at gathering together the small units of oral tradition (vignettes of Christ's life and sayings), and lastly the actual work of our Evangelists. This whole process was under the guidance of the Church, who applied, while she transmitted, the message of Christ to her ever-increasing needs.

If our ghost of Christian ages past should interpose at this point to remind us that an ancient colleague of his, Papias, rather clearly states that "Mark, having become the interpreter of Peter, wrote down accurately everything that he remembered", we should have to tell him that Peter's sermons followed a plan and contained matter which was common to the preaching of the primitive Church. Mark, with him in Rome, would have obtained such material for his Gospel, and not the least advantage of his being with Peter is the peculiar quince-like sharpness of his report. Peter had been an eyewitness of what had passed. However, this did not render

Mark insensitive to other source material available in the Church, nor did it preclude him from exercising his own powers in the composition of his Gospel.

When we come to examine Mark's message we must be aware of what the above briefly sketched discussions have contributed. The "Jesus-of-history" movement may be closed—but it has given us a greater appreciation of the historical factor to be considered in the Gospels even if, unfortunately, it overemphasized this to the detriment of the real significance of Christ. The Synoptic Problem may not be solved—but it has underlined the points of comparison and contrast between Matthew, Mark and Luke. Form criticism may have been marred by manifold defects (its inability to see the Church as preserving, not manufacturing, Christ's teaching, for example)—but it has asked important questions about the formation of the Gospels and has shown us how the Gospel was steeped in the living stream of the Church's life.

We may now move on to look more closely at that message.

Dramatic narrative

We are accustomed to being told of the rugged, richly descriptive style of Mark, a Gospel which is nothing if not alive, real. We are carried back to the lakeside towns of Galilee, meet their inhabitants, sense the bustling but often humdrum life of the time of Christ. Compared with Matthew, Mark gives many more details, a greater characterization, in recording the same events. We might align the healing of the man sick of the palsy (Mark 2.1–12 and Matt. 9.1–8), the episode of the Gerasene demoniacs (Mark 5.1–20 and Matt. 8.28–34), the raising of the daughter of Jairus (Mark 5.21–43 and Matt. 9.18–26), the healing of many sick folk (Mark 7.24–37 and Matt. 15.29–31)—where Mark devotes one-half of his space to describing the healing of a deaf-mute. In reading Mark (if we close our ears to his nerve-racking repetitions of "and", "immediately", "do", "have") it is not too difficult for us to become the enthralled audience of an interesting if not an expert raconteur who, with a minimum of comment, allows events to speak for themselves. We are in the presence of the first Christian dramatist.

Now this dramatic quality of Mark serves a purpose which deserves more attention than it has often received. True, philologists and grammarians have been distressingly thorough when analyzing Mark's style, but the concrete realism of the account has yet to be made to surrender its full worth. Why is there that emphasis on living reality, on actions rather than words, on events rather than on their explanation? Surely it was because Mark's sources were still mesmerized by the impact of what had happened, still dazed by the encounter with Christ amid the circumstances of everyday life. Revelation and salvation in the Old Testament were given tied to a people's history; this could be no less so for the fulfilment of that revelation, of that salvation, in Christ. Consciously or unconsciously, Mark was heir to the practices of the past. The scenario of man's meeting with Christ is drawn in situations of such palpable domesticity that his coming is seen to be graven on the rough stone of human history.

Structure of the apostolic preaching: its use in Mark

Mark, then, in the very décor of his drama is preparing the background for his reader's encounter with Christ. When we come to examine the plan of his Gospel, this becomes even more apparent. We have already remarked that Mark (like the other Synoptists) owes a debt to that primitive preaching which proclaimed the Good News of salvation in the primitive Church, and this debt is to be extended not only to the matter which was common to such preaching but also to the overall presiding plan, which was constructed with a wonderful economy. As we have remarked in Chapter 1, from the descriptions of the actual preaching of the Apostles as recorded in Acts and the Epistles of St Paul, we can arrive with some certainty at this primitive message. It may be presented thus:

The prophecies are fulfilled, the new age has dawned.

The Messiah, of the House of David, has come.

He is Jesus of Nazareth, who
    was baptized by John
    did mighty works by the power of God
    suffered and died for us
    rose from the dead
    was exalted at God's right hand
    will come again in judgement.

Repent and be baptized for the forgiveness of sin.

Now, while the passion and resurrection of Christ are the basis of this preaching of the Apostles, the earthly ministry of Christ is referred to because in that ministry are already manifested the signs of God's inauguration of the last times. The ministry, therefore, enters into the salvific context of the Passion and Resurrection.

When we turn to Mark it is easy to see that his Gospel is simply an expansion of that apostolic preaching. He begins (as does this *kerygma*) with the fulfilment of prophecy and goes on to describe John's baptism of Jesus. The following six chapters show Christ performing the mighty works of God. The latter third of Mark's Gospel gives in great detail the story of his passion and death and concludes with the Resurrection. Interspersed among the various incidents of the opening pages of the Gospel are appeals to repent.

These doctrinal foundations are evidently of paramount importance. We should accord them an attention that does not waver in favour of seeking a biography of Christ, with a restlessness to discover a chronological and geographical plan of his life. Too much energy has been dissipated on these quests. Matthew, Mark and Luke do offer us a skeleton outline of Christ's ministry; in Galilee, in journeys afield, in Jerusalem, with incidents that took place in each locality. That such a framework corresponds to facts need not be laboured and that it afforded a neat means for offering the doctrine involved in those facts must be evident. Yet an over-concern for a "Life of Jesus" obscures the primary interest of the early preaching and of our Evangelists: to pass on Christ's teaching.

Preoccupation with a chronological and geographical ordering of Mark's Gospel has had another diversionary effect. We have not always appreciated what can only be called the build-up of his matter. The focal point of the Gospel was to present, as we have mentioned, the person of Christ. While using the material and schema of the primitive preaching, Mark laid out his materials in such a way that we can see a twofold process at work in Christ's manifestation of his role.

From ch. 1.1 to ch. 8.26, by amassing diverse episodes in which Christ is constantly effecting wonders by word and deed, he gives a cumulative impression of the significance of that ministry. Incident after incident—healings, exorcisms, authoritative pronouncements—are marshalled together to give a well-defined sense that *somebody* has invaded this world. This first part of the Gospel reaches a climax in Caesarea Philippi when Peter confesses to Jesus, "Thou art the Christ." The second part of the Gospel moves forward in this acknowledgement of Jesus as Messiah. It contains three great sections: ch. 8.27 to ch. 10.52, which tells of Christ's journeying to Jerusalem and which is dominated by the announcement of the Passion and Resurrection; chapters 11 to 13, which tell us of the ministry in Jerusalem day by day but with a grouping of material which is primarily literary and thematic (rather than chronological)—we have the five

conflicts of Jesus with the Jews; chapters 14 to
16, dealing with the Passion and Resurrection,
are obviously designed as the apogee of the
Gospel. In fine, Mark has not neglected to lead
us on gradually in a growing understanding of
the mission of Jesus, and in so doing has given
us a Christology.

Mark's Christology: Son of Man—

The very disposition of the Second Gospel
with the predominance of the Passion narrative
indicates that Mark wants to show us a crucified
Messiah as the realization of the promise of God
to his people. Christ is the victorious Saviour, not
despite his sufferings and humiliations but
through them. This double theme of humiliation and glory is resumed in the title constantly
used in the Gospels for Christ: Son of Man. It is
generally agreed that the use of this title in the
Gospels recognizes an historical attitude of
Christ; he employed it to designate his mission.
Some fourteen times it is found on his lips in
Mark, and outside its use on two occasions as a
claim to authority (Mark 2.10—"the Son of Man
has power on earth to forgive sins"—and Mark
2.28—"the Son of Man is Lord of the sabbath
also"), we can perceive in it a prophetic designa-
tion which speaks of the rejection of Christ or
foretells his future glory. The depth of doctrine

this title covers cannot be overestimated—in it are contained the seeds of a whole Christology. How can we learn this? By placing it in the explanatory context which Mark and the primitive Church gave it, the context of the Old Testament with all the atmosphere which surrounded it in the last years before the coming of Christ.

Our theology manuals have demonstrated that, in evaluating the riches contained in revelation, a process has been set up wherein theological reasoning has played an important part. A baptized Aristotelianism has been made to subserve revelation (too often, we must confess, exaggeratedly). But Mark was no scholastic; his thought-patterns were not those of Greek philosophy. A Jew, his mind and his theology (if this is not an anachronism)—as well as those of his sources—were formed by the Old Testament. To understand and convey the salvific meaning of an event meant, for him, to immerse it in the Old Testament from which it emerged clarified. This was most obviously the case for the Christ-Event, but here, not only was this explained by reference to the Old Testament; it, in turn, illumined that ancient revelation. As the Anglican divine, A. G. Hebert, has remarked, "Old Testament prophecies run to Christ as tidal rivers to the sea, only to feel his reflex influence upon them." It will be with no surprise, therefore, that we can trace some seventy-one quotations from the Old Testament in Mark's small Gospel, a calculation which does not exhaust his employment of it—there are numerous allusions underlying the text. The primitive Church was expressing its awareness of Christ in a thought-pattern which was woven in threads from its sacred writings. And in so doing it was following the path blazed by Christ, who transfigured the older hopes in himself and declared his mission against the background of Old-Testament thought. Christ's coming was a direct descent from above, yet the ground had been prepared by a task force through which revelation had penetrated history.

If we try to define what was the most important Old-Testament element in Mark we must readily acknowledge that it was the messianic expectation, but a messianic hope that was polarized around two visions: the present, persecuted age and the coming age of glory. The ideas circulating in the time of Christ have the theme of the agonizing distance between Jewish circumstances now and the promised spiritual reality to come. Apocalyptic literature, canonical and apocryphal (as the Dead Sea Scrolls testify), is concerned with revealing the future glory, the revelation (*apocalypsis*) of a mystery. It is precisely this context which surrounds the problematical Chapter 13 of Mark. There we find that

Christ has resumed those two Ages in himself, the Son of Man. His humiliation and glory, his present coming in suffering and his future coming in glory are intimately linked with the great "secret" of apocalyptic; indeed, the most optimistic hopes of this latter are exceeded. That vision of apocalyptists, that ideal of the whole of the Old Testament, God's permanent presence with man, is now a reality. It is in this perspective, too, that St Paul's "mystery of revelation" will be seen: it is not a series of mysteries, but the revelation of a unique mystery, of *the* mystery. It is not one or other detail of the divine plan, but that which is its foundation and explanation. The great "secret" is not something but some*one*— Christ.

In that "little Apocalypse" of Chapter 13 Mark has reassumed the Danielic figure of the Son of Man. In Chapter 7 of the Book of Daniel we have a symbolic representation of the drama of world history. The great powers pass before our eyes; then "one like a son of man" takes over their empires and rules for ever. This old symbol of the final victory of the spiritual forces, of good over evil, of God himself over all that would oppose his will, is shown by Mark to be Christ. The Jewish hope of their own saviour is realized in *this* Son of Man.

But if Daniel has emphasized the glorious coming of this saviour, less patently has he sketched his humiliation, a clear trait of Christ in the Gospels. For this we have to go back once more to the Old Testament, to the latter half of the Book of Isaiah. There we find another side to the awaited Hope of Israel: he is to suffer, and through those sufferings make expiation for his people. Christ, then, fused into one the ancient images of a glorious Son of Man, conquering evil and reigning for ever, and of the Suffering Servant of God who, through his reparatory suffering, effects salvation. In the second part of Mark's Gospel both these characteristics of Christ are never far from the surface. If Mark sometimes seems to make a secret of this messianic office of Christ, if Christ himself would impose silence on those who would proclaim his messiahship—on the demons, on those healed by him, even on the Apostles themselves—this was because the mystery which was in the process of being revealed needed to be mediated slowly to the minds of men, for the Messiah, the one whose role was to liberate man, was God.

—And Son of God

During the course of Christ's ministry, despite the wonders he worked, it remains doubtful whether any of the Apostles understood his divinity. Only after the Resurrection could there be that certitude. However, the sayings and deeds of Christ during that ministry were a preparation for the moment of truth. After the Resurrection the Apostles, looking back at those incidents of Christ's life, could see how everything was so clear now, how everything fell into place. The ministry was seen in its true perspective, the acts of the Son of God. This title, used sparingly in Mark, shows an acknowledgement of Christ's divinity only by the world of the spirit during his lifetime— the demons recognize his divinity, heaven itself acclaims it in the Baptism and Transfiguration; but man cannot yet know it until Christ has ended his life, his mission accomplished. Yet when Mark wrote his Gospel, Christ's divinity was known by the primitive Church and it is in this light that we are expected to read it—"The Gospel of Jesus Christ, the Son of God". (Mark. 1.1.) We have been forewarned and can watch the drama knowing what the outcome will be.

This pedagogy which is a characteristic of the whole of revelation, this gradual leading on of men to understand and appreciate the divine message, is nowhere more evident than in the revelation of what Christ was. A rigorous Jewish monotheism could not easily suspect that God's Word would be his Son, despite the help afforded in this direction by the Wisdom writings of old; the ancient apocalypses never dreamt that their age of glory would be effected through a Son of Man who was in absolute truth Son of God. And it was only with the Resurrection that that pedagogy was completed.

Confronted with Christ

Mark, then, offers us principally a meeting with the person of Christ. Unlike Matthew or Luke, his fellow Synoptists, he does not wish to give us an extended teaching of Christ, but would concentrate on confronting us with him. He does this in a most realistic fashion, showing how closely Christ was part of our history, yet will make us aware to what summit revelation is reaching in the Mystery that was Christ. He will have us, like Christ himself, reach out from history into the limitless horizon of faith, from the abjectly human to the gloriously divine, a divinity which was no chilly abstraction but a living presence encountered by men. Mark's Christology is designed not so much to indoctrinate us as to confront us with Christ, challenge us to respond to his mission. Mark may well have been ignorant of the theological niceties surrounding the Hypostatic Union, the modality of the Redemption, the triple grace of Christ. But we too frequently have lost ourselves in intellectual explorations in the margin of such truths, hypnotized by ideas on Christ rather than inspired by his person. Mark holds out to us a means of correcting that diversion; his signpost points to a rendezvous with Christ.

ST MATTHEW'S MESSAGE

Matthew's method

IT might not be too irreverent to suggest that
the parting advice given to graduating exegetes
in the schools of Christian antiquity was "Write
a scroll on St Matthew's Gospel". The law of
supply and demand would have justified such a
proposal; any investigation we care to make of
the use of St Matthew in the ancient Church
shows that it was the most cited Gospel. Ignatius,
Clement, the *Didache*, employed it freely; Justin
Martyr quotes it no less than 170 times; St John
Chrysostom contributed some 90 homilies on its
texts. So blind was the early enthusiasm of the
heretical Ebionites for it that they resolutely
refused to recognize any other Gospel. In the
Middle Ages, moreover, the authors of the *Com-
mentaries on the Sentences* and the *Summas*
knew it for good source-material. Later centuries
showed no diminishing of interest in the First
Gospel, and whatever way we take it, Renan
was surely right when he described Matthew as
"the Evangelist of the Church". It was only in
more recent times that, among independent

critics, Matthew's significance receded before that of Mark.

If we enquire into the cause for this centuries-long interest in Matthew we shall find that it lies in two aspects of this Gospel: its lengthy presentation of Christ's teaching with its numerous applications to the everyday life of the Christian, and its systematization. Matthew has succeeded very well in organizing the various points of Christ's teaching so that we are offered, in five great tableaux, effective groupings of similar material. This has meant, obviously, joining sayings, sermons and parables together that were delivered at different times, with small regard for their time and place of origin. In Matthew the notion of "seeing" is sufficient to link up Christ's sayings on "Whosoever shall look on a woman . . ." and "If thy right eye scandalize thee . . ."; the connection is logical rather than chronological or geographical. Another attractive Matthean touch is noticeable in his numerical groupings; we have the use of the number "seven" which, while possibly containing a certain symbolism, seems to have been employed to facilitate memorizing. There are seven beatitudes, seven petitions in the *Our Father*, seven parables, seven "Woes" against the Pharisees, seven demons who return, seven loaves, seven baskets, pardon to be given "till seventy times seven times". There is even the woman who had seven husbands. We can also detect in Matthew other procedures which make for a Gospel which is orderly (this did not escape Papias, that Master of the Rolls), memorable (the Gospel texts which come most easily even to our own lips are, more likely than not, Matthew's), and which gives Christ's teaching at some length.

Christ as teacher

But it is precisely this last point which has aroused the ire of a number of non-Catholic scholars. Aware as they are that various situations in the early life of the Church made for the transmitting of the Gospel message, it has seemed to them sometimes that the figure of Christ has been obscured by that message; that what we are being given is not so much Christ but the pre-occupations of the Church. It is suggested that Matthew (and Luke) are substituting a teaching which announced and described the mighty acts of God—in place of that Christ of St Mark, whose life, death and resurrection *was* the action of God. It is understandable, we are told, that Matthew (and Luke) would improve Mark's grammar, remove odd words, prune his narratives. Some discomfort begins to be felt when it is noticed that the word "gospel", which in Mark is the Christ-Event itself, begins to signify in the other Synoptists the good tidings of the Kingdom. But this disquiet turns into intense irritation when Matthew starts to supply discourses where Mark was content to describe Christ as performing the works of his ministry.

Yet the interesting thing is that on the occasions when Matthew does include his massive discourse material, each discourse is offered us at a point where the Marcan narrative requires some such teaching. In fact, Matthew is availing himself of sources which were already there but which Mark, due to his own particular aim of presenting the stark figure of Christ itself, neglected. We shall find that Mark often records that Christ taught—even that on some ten occasions he was addressed as "Teacher", and that his audience was astounded at his teaching. But repeatedly, when Mark so describes Christ, he gives little indication of what he taught. Mark will tell us that Christ customarily used parables, but he offers only two extended examples of this. Mark, then, no less than Matthew or Luke, had at hand the teaching of Christ, but sacrificed this to direct attention to the person of Jesus. Matthew, however, giving us the teaching of Christ, does so, not because he conceived the notion of Jesus as "Teacher", but because the teaching of Christ was part and parcel of his messianic role.

There is one further introductory remark to be made on this concern of Matthew to give us Christ's teaching: it is directed also to giving us a greater understanding of the mystery of Christ. There is an attempt to paint in the background to the Person encountered in Mark. To take two examples, we might consider the scenes of the baptism of Christ and the confession of Peter at Caesarea Philippi. In Mark we have the austere account of Christ being baptized by John the Baptist. The question was bound to rise unbidden to the lips of the primitive Christians, Why should the sinless Christ be baptized? Matthew will offer us the answer in the form of a brief conversation between Christ and the Baptist: "It is well that we should thus fulfil all due observance." And not only does this answer explain Christ's action; it serves also to point the way for Christian practices. In Matt. 16.13–20, we have the account of Peter's recognition of Jesus as Messiah. Comparing Matthew's text with that of the other Synoptists, we find that Matthew has included two major additions: the recognition by Peter that Christ was the Son of God and the conferring of the primacy on Peter. Matthew has legitimately dovetailed in one triptych the three companion pictures of Peter's confession of Christ's messiahship, his later perfect realization of who Christ was and the conferring of the primacy on Peter by Christ. So it is that at a glance, as it were, we learn of Christ's divine mission extended through the world *via* the Church whose primate is Peter. Matthew will have us aware of yet another dimension to the life and work of Jesus.

Fulfilment of the Old Testament

We may now move on to examine what is that teaching of Christ which Matthew has written up for us in his Gospel. It has been proposed that Matthew's Gospel is an apologia for Christ, constant references being made to the Old Testament to defend Jesus and his mission from would-be Jewish attackers. Matthew would have been the first Christian apologist, the initiator of the apologetic method where exposition of a doctrine takes second place to defence of that doctrine. Now, while certain apologetic tendencies can be noted in Matthew's account, it is surely exaggerated to say that this was his primary intention. The Gospel is rather a proclamation than a defence. It has also been suggested that Matthew's teaching is the doctrine of the fulfilment of the Old Testament in Christ. He makes a continual use of the Old Testament to underscore Christ's words and deeds as fulfilling the ancient expectation; Christ was the climax of the whole history of

Israel. On something like a dozen occasions, Matthew explicitly asserts that the Scriptures of old were "fulfilled" in Jesus and his mission. Even the new order established by Christ will maintain and perfect the elements of Old-Testament revelation and morality, "fulfilling" them. Yet, once more, while this is most certainly true, it is not the all-central message of Matthew but rather one aspect of it. That which gives Matthew its bulky contribution to the story of revelation is its message on the invasion of this world by the Kingdom of God. The importance of this contribution cannot be overestimated and it is not too much to ask that we investigate it in some detail. We may do this by opening our discussion with an examination of the notion of the Kingdom of God and then proceed to enquire how Matthew has treated the Kingdom in its three principal themes of the presence of God among men, the Church as the form God's rule among them will take and, lastly, the New Law as the norm which determines entrance to and existence in that kingdom.

The Kingdom of God

Even the least alert reader cannot fail to catch some significance in Matthew's constant employment of the words "Kingdom", "Kingdom of Heaven," "Kingdom of God". It is unfortunate

that the word "Kingdom" in these expressions
is misleading for us. It conjures up primarily the
idea of a realm or order of society inaugurated
by God. This is not the basic conception, which
is expressed rather by the Hebrew word *malkuth*
—the active *rule* of God. The sovereignty of God
in the hearts and lives of men, as shown by their
doing of his will, describes the fundamental content of what Christ meant by the Kingdom of
God. It is his actual dominion, his royal rule.
Such dominion, such kingship, implies a domain,
a society in which that rule is effective. But the
essential emphasis is upon God's dominion.

Now the notion of God's dominion over man
is such that it recapitulates many other biblical
ideas and is, indeed, at the core of the Bible's
message. The truth is that this dominion of God
is as extensive as his work, including in itself all
the divine overtures to man; he wants men to
recognize one fact: They are his already. The
sovereignty of God is therefore, in some way, the
point of departure for all revealed religion. God
will establish a rule over the hearts and minds
of men that has been rightly his since creation.
This dominion may be manifested when he reveals himself in the awe-inspiring theophanies of
old, or when he comes in secret to the soul of
man. In other words, the Kingdom of God means

simply the effective role of God in man's existence, and it demands recognition.

It was the ancient hope of the old dispensation that God would come and rule the world in power, exercising a dominion over all—even over those who would subtract themselves from such an influence. While, in the oldest vocabulary of Israel, we fail to detect any royal title applied to God, we do find that the people were ruled by the invisible Presence of God from the Ark, manifested by the tablets of the Law and the sceptre it contained. Yahweh was God of throne and altar. When David and Solomon ruled in glory from Jerusalem, God's rule began to be described in terms borrowed from royal pageantry—He was "King", with a royal rule over a "Kingdom", his people. Later, the Prophets widened the conception of God's rule to include his lordship over history and over the interminable empires which were successfully subjugating his people. But the same prophets warned their hearers that the awaited universal dominion of God would favour the Chosen Race only if that race repented of its continual defections from God's covenant. Right conduct it was rather than race that was the differential for peaceful possession under the Rule of God. With the return from the Exile, when apocalyptic piety gave a new lease of life to the Jewish spirit,

we find the most illuminating texts to explain
Matthew's doctrine of the Kingdom. Dan. 7.13–14,
27 marks the decisive transition from the concept of an earthly to a heavenly kingdom in a
hope that reached unprecedented intensity.
This kingdom would embrace heaven and earth,
time and eternity. It is nothing strange to find
that Christ employed, while complementing and
perfecting, those royal categories of Daniel to
indicate the fulfilment of the divine work.

The Presence of God

When we turn to Matthew we find the first
theme of the Kingdom announced in the Infancy
Narrative: the Presence of God among men. The
account of the genealogy and birth of Jesus is
designed to set him in his rightful place in
history, in the history of salvation. He is the last
link in the long history of deliverances offered
by God to his people. And the account of the
birth of Jesus warns us at the same time that it
was a new departure, in fact the invasion of this
world by a new creation of God. The emphatic
words of the whole story of the infancy of Jesus
are those taken from the Old Testament: "They
shall call his name Emmanuel, which is, God
with us." The ancient hope of Israel, the
shekinah, God's glorious presence, is with men.

But it is not, as so often in the Old Testament, a transitory presence. The concluding words of the Gospel of St Matthew echo these earlier ones: "I am with you always even to the consummation of the world." His Gospel is polarized between these two texts; he will tell us how, through the life, ministry, death and resurrection of Christ, the presence of God is with men —always. This time, there is no temporary visitation.

No longer would men have to turn to the past, to the theocratic ideal of the Israelite monarchy. Their King was present to them for ever. The old personal anthropomorphisms expressing God's ruling presence fell pitifully below this new reality. The divine dominion was actualized in a manner preceding generations had not even dimly perceived; in the deeds of his ministry Christ showed that the Rule of God was now beginning. In fact, Christ is not so much the inaugurator of this sovereignty of God as in himself that power, that kingdom; in the words of Origen, he is the *auto-basileia*.

But there is something else, something of unusual importance, to be grafted on to the old concept of God's ruling presence; with Christ, the eternal and heavenly empire of Daniel is enriched by a mystical content: the presence of

God with men invites them into a particular relationship with him in Christ—a society of believers united intimately with God. We are face to face with the second element of the Kingdom of God upon earth, the first-fruits of that kingdom, that rule of God: the Church, the domain in which the sovereignty of God will be most realistically recognized.

It is for the instruction and guidance of this people of God that Matthew has so extensively recorded the teaching of Christ. In fact, if we place ourselves at the standpoint of that community, the Church, which embodies the presence of God, we shall be best able to appreciate the trend of Matthew's thought. What is that teaching of Christ, those instructions which govern life in the Church, under the kingdom or rule of God? Matthew has given us the answer in five "books" in his Gospel. While using (like Mark) the geographical plan of Christ's work— his ministry in Galilee, his journeys, his passion, death and resurrection in Jerusalem—Matthew (again like Mark) has superimposed theological preoccupations on this plan, but this time it is a "systematic theology" of the Kingdom in its most challenging form, the Church. We find that Matthew follows a well-established Old-Testament precedent, most clearly discernible in the

Pentateuch, of giving his teaching strung, as it were, between narrative sections.

The Inauguration of the Kingdom

After the two opening chapters on the birth of Christ (which define the perspective in which the whole Gospel is to be read—the divine presence among men) Matthew launches into his Gospel of the Kingdom. Chapters 3 and 4 are an account of Christ's work in Galilee and are designed to stake a claim on our interest in the ministry, the inauguration of the Kingdom of God. Then follows (in chapters 5 to 7) Matthew's report of the manifesto of the Kingdom, the lengthy Sermon on the Mount. This comprehensive survey of the principal points of Christ's teaching is the document of naturalization for the Kingdom of God, the new contract between the interested parties of God and man; in a word, the New Covenant. Such is its significance that we must return to it later.

The Power of the Kingdom

Chapters 8 and 9 give us a series of miracles, nine in all—a miracle-cycle—each three of which are separated by two short sayings of Christ which are directed to show the ultimate horizons of Christ's work: the acts of the Messiah. What is underlined is not so much the role of Christ as wonderworker as the fulfilment of his messianic

mission. By these deeds Christ manifests the
power of God over nature, sickness, death and
demons. The Kingdom is present, the rule of
God is felt, in the person and works of Christ—
especially in his exorcisms and works of healing
which intimately attack the rule and consequences of sin. This same power is communi-
cated to the disciples when they are sent to
preach the Kingdom, and we can see from the
Acts of the Apostles (2.22) how the power of
miracles is considered a credential of the missionary. As "Jesus went about the whole of
Galilee, *teaching* in their synagogues . . . and
curing every kind of disease and infirmity"
(Matthew's summarizing formula, 4.23, and
9.35, for Christ's work), so too the disciples will
similarly extend the Kingdom by their preaching and miracles.

Chapter 10 offers instructions for those mis-
sionaries. Like the Sermon on the Mount, this
missionary discourse is an amalgam of various
sayings of Christ. Mark's short mission discourse
to the Twelve (Mark 6.6–13) and Luke's discourse to the seventy-two disciples are joined with
other related sayings to form Matthew's exhorta-
tion of Christ's missionary teaching in its full
application. Not only to the Twelve or to the
seventy-two, but to all disciples of the Kingdom
is this given. The perspective of persecution (in

Matt. 10.17–25) is larger than that of the first
mission. There is food for thought here for all
members of the Church called to suffer persecution and difficulties in their work for Christ.

The Mystery of the Kingdom

The third great section of Matthew deals with
the mystery of the Kingdom, the problems of its
members, its growth, its final consummation.
This stretches from chapters 11 to 13, and it is
in this chapter 13, after the customary accounts
of the deeds of Christ, that we find Matthew's
long plan of the parables.

The parables are perhaps the most characteristic trait in the recorded teaching of Christ in the
Gospels; their imaginative treatment of doctrinal issues assured a secure place for them in
the mind of tradition. (Also, for our own interest, it has been pointed out that little else
from antiquity gives us such a picture of small-
town provincial life in the Roman Palestine of
the time of the Gospels.)

Christ made use of the parable for the purpose
of describing the Kingdom of God: the various
responses to its first overtures, the success and
failure of its reception (the Sower, 13.3–9,18–
23); the coexistence of good and bad within it
and the ever-present warning of the final sifting
(the Wheat and the Cockle, 13.24–30,36–43);

the certainty of its coming and its development
(the Mustard Seed, 13.31–2); the inner power
and efficacy of the Kingdom (the Leaven, 13.
33); its supreme importance for men (the Hidden
Treasure, 13.44, the Pearl of Great Price, 45–6),
and finally the eschatological mystery, the consummation of the Kingdom (the Dragnet, 13.47–
50). We may complement this picture of the
Kingdom by adding additional parables which
Matthew includes in the later chapters of his
Gospel: the grace of the Kingdom offered to all
(20.1–15;22.1–14); the need to be prepared for
its coming (24.45–51;25.1–13,14–30). We shall
find that perhaps the line of thought which receives the greatest emphasis in this parable treatment of the Kingdom is the sense of immediacy
fluctuating with a coming threat; the fall of
Jerusalem was not too far distant, and its dangerous shadow cast shades over the lives of those
who were experiencing a confrontation with the
Kingdom of God. They had to hurry. The
eschatological significance of that fall could not
be neglected by later Christians; they too did
not know the day nor the hour. They too had
to decide in favour of all the demands of the
Kingdom.

The Church

The fourth great section of Matthew deals

with those first-fruits of the Kingdom, the Church. It is not without its importance that the major passages in this section are found not in the discourse section of Chapter 18 but in the accounts of Christ's deeds. We have the announcement of the foundation of the Church and Peter's primacy in 16.13–20, in a context which shows that the Church is founded through the suffering of Christ; it was no idle systematization of Matthew that connected the sayings of Christ on the Church with the three predictions of the Passion.

In the "ecclesiastical" discourse of Chapter 18 Matthew is content to confine himself to offering the teaching of Jesus on the relations of Christians to each other. After the powerful themes of the parables and the heavy doctrine of Chapter 16, Matthew, almost with relief, turns to domestic problems, paying particular attention to the avoidance of scandal and fraternal correction.

The Kingdom at hand

In his final section, Matthew deals with the vital fact, demanding undeviating commitment, that the Kingdom of God is at hand. After a narrative section in which, more than in any other, he offers various sayings of Christ, the Evangelist gives us the great eschatological discourse in chapters 24 and 25. Two perspectives command this matter: the fall of Jerusalem and the end of the world. It is very likely that in the preaching of Christ these two horizons were clearly separated. But in Matthew the two perspectives are fused rather than juxtaposed. This is not without its theological significance; for if we may distinguish chronologically the two events, yet the second is prefigured in the first. The judgement on the Chosen Race will be echoed by God's judgement on the world. More than any earlier intervention of God in the human story, this visitation merits the expressions and imagery of the prophetical "Day of Yahweh"—wars, famines, unparalleled suffering, cosmic catastrophes. The ultimate manifestation of God's power will herald the consummation of the Kingdom. No more will his rule be baulked by the waywardness of his creatures.

Matthew has laid it clearly before his readers that they must choose their own destiny in face of such a sure hope of God's victory. The Christian life may be lived under terrifying dangers and fraught with temptation; but God's influence directing their lives ensures every encouragement to maintain their steadfastness and responsibility before him.

The New Law

To offer a guide by which Christians could

direct their conduct in the Kingdom of God, had not Matthew already given Jesus' teaching in the Sermon on the Mount? Here was the New Law, given to the disciples in the presence of the multitude—as intended primarily for those who would undertake to enter the Kingdom, but indeed as the only law that could direct the lives of all men. As Moses on Sinai had given his people their highway code to God, so too Christ, from another mount, had proclaimed another and greater law. In that Sermon on the Mount Christ had laid down the precepts which govern the principal situations of man. Matthew has presented us with this compilation of various aspects of Christ's teaching—the spirit which animates those entering the Kingdom of God, the perfecting of the laws and practices of Judaism on four chief scores—the fifth, sixth, second and seventh commandments; detachment from riches and consequently freedom from their ever-threatening downward drag; relations with our neighbours, the acid test of our relations with God; finally, the challenge of the Kingdom and the response we are called upon to make—submission to God's dominion.

The attentive reader of the Sermon on the Mount is forced to ask himself questions about his situation, about even his most ordinary day-to-day circumstances in the pattern of salvation.

Is God's influence impeded in any aspect of his existence, is his co-operation with God's will all it might be? True, the Sermon places ideals before us and our constant striving may never effect our reaching them. But those ideals are possible and are both a stimulus to further efforts and a criticism of what we have already achieved. In spite of all, the presence of God prevents discouragement.

The last word

It is not unexpected to find in St Matthew's Gospel, so orderly in so many other respects, that his final verses give us a summary of his message: "Going, therefore, *teach* ye all nations, *baptizing* them in the name of the Father, and of the Son and of the Holy Ghost. And, behold, *I am with you all days* . . ." The three basic elements of the Kingdom of God, the three great props of the Old Testament, are linked together with a nice economy. The Law, now the new law of Christ, which instructs men unto justice; the People of God, now that new people, the Church, united in faith and love to Father, Son and Spirit by baptism; lastly, the Presence of God with man, formerly transitory, now permanent in the Church—all these underlie that baptismal formula. What was for the men of old a dream is, for us, a common birthright.

5

ST LUKE'S MESSAGE

The humanism of Luke

AMONG all the New Testament documents, none gives us more convincingly an atmosphere of early Christian humanism than the Gospel of St Luke. Here we have an attempt by a Hellenist, a man of letters, to present, in its most attractive features, the message of Christianity to a world which had known Hellenistic culture in all its forms. In sharp contrast to both Matthew and Mark, Luke exhibits a disposition of mind which was already an asset in grasping the worldwide dimensions of the Christ-Event, its implications for the lights and shadows of the human situation. They would have to learn the hard way (as did Peter himself) that the Jewish pattern of life was only one facet of existence; Luke, however, by his very education, was immersed in a culture which was a natural preparation for the universalism of Christ. And this universalism, this recognition of the validity of Christ's message for all men, rested on another assumption: that all were equal in the sight of God. This answered too to the better trends in a

Greek philosophy stretched over the Mediter-
ranean basin—that the individual had his significance. The interplay of the Jewish notion of
race "solidarity" and the Hellenistic one of the
value of the individual set up a tension which
only Christ could resolve. Luke, again, had something startling to offer his non-Jewish contemporaries. Finally, in a world which was torn
between an optimism born of the realization
that both man and matter were basically good,
and a pessimism which a sorry history of
humanity had sponsored, Luke was able to explain that the much-sought-after Saviour had
come to reinstate the right order of things. The
Word of God had entered a bright world dark-
ened by sin; this time, not as the creative Word
but as the redeeming Word—the Word that sets
men free. The thinking man need no longer be
dismayed at the vitiating process history constantly heralded; God had made all things new.

Paul may have been desperately concerned
to mediate this message to his Gentile hearers,
but it is in Luke that we find such a message
tied, as it were, to the very encounter of Christ
in the streets and homes of Palestine. The pulsing immediacy of Paul's message to the Gentiles
would seem, if we may so put it, to have left
neither time nor space to link it intimately with
those scenes from the life of Christ which so

touchingly illustrated such hope for humanity. But Luke, historian, doctor, humanist, with his appreciation of the civilized life of his time, his consciousness of its problems (the opposition between rich and poor, the contrast of cosmopolitanism and nationalism—is the situation so greatly changed today?—the despised social position of women), and lastly, his human sympathy with those whom the world judged too harshly, was eminently endowed to portray to Christian hearers God's love and understanding of man, so delicately manifested in Christ.

It will not be surprising, then, if we can detect a duality in the Third Gospel, the work of a sensitive and cultured mind now Christian, the opus of a *littérateur* become evangelist. Such a duality may be discerned, for example, in the four opening verses of his Gospel. There we find that the conventions of profane history-writing have been made to subserve the Christian account. He may refer to "events"—but those that have taken place among us; to "tradition"—but of the Christian transmission; to "eyewitnesses" —but of that first preaching of the Gospel; to "instructed"—but by the primitive catechesis; to "certainty"—but to that now provided by the report Luke is introducing.

We must beware, however, of reading into this prologue an expectation of ours that Luke has not promised to satisfy. He has alerted us to a history of the beginnings of Christianity, but he has not committed himself to writing a biography of Christ. His concern is to give us the salvific meaning of Christ's words and deeds, rather than draw up a catalogue of events (as, indeed, we may well expect from an Evangelist).

Luke's aim of bridgebuilding between the two worlds of rugged Judaism and polished Hellenism will lead him to present his message in a fashion that is designed to evoke the greatest response in his readers. His Greek, if not classical, is still cast in the mould of a good, widely used *koine*, the common use of which by educated men of that time (as well as by the populace) warns us against labelling it "vulgar". Questions of purely local Palestinian customs he will omit or explain. Accounts of Gospel episodes and sayings of Christ which are common to the three Synoptists he will often report in his own way, adding or omitting nuances in view of those same readers. We shall see also that much of the matter peculiar to Luke himself will stress a content in Christianity that will have an immediate appeal to the finer sentiments of his Greek contemporaries.

How may we, whose problems mirror those of that earlier, if less sophisticated age, define that message of Luke in a period when common cultures clash even within the cloister of Christendom? We may do this by examining his teaching under three headings which summarize the perspectives which have directed Luke's work. There is first of all the "new life" which is made available to men through the exalted Christ. Next, the missionary consciousness of the primitive Church saw the significance of this and recognized how utterly universal Christ's Church was to become. Lastly, there is, in Christ's words and deeds, his contacts with the strikingly contrasted persons found in Luke's Gospel, a sign of God's care for the individual soul, a divine acknowledgement of its supreme value.

New life

It has been brought home to us that under the Gospel accounts we can feel the pulse of the life of the primitive Church, sense its coursing bloodstream building up and renewing the existence of man. The Evangelists, in a way, have put that life into our hands. Now while this is evident in Matthew and Mark, it is evident in a different way with Luke. Matthew and Mark give us more markedly the atmosphere contemporaneous with the words and deeds they recount, but Luke has brought something of the *euphoria* of the primitive Church into his story, something of that

expanding sense of freedom which exhilarated
the Church after Pentecost. This derived from
the realization that the long-awaited new age had
arrived in power. This was the age of God, of
his Son, Jesus Christ, their exalted Lord, of his
mighty wonderworker, the Holy Spirit, who was
drastically effecting a renewal of life in a sin-
drugged humanity. The whole Church was the
centre of gravity for this new dynamism which
was to re-create the world. Such a breakthrough
showed those on the fringes of Judaism that
existence need no longer be a treadmill of des-
pair; history did not go round in vicious circles
but ran its appointed course according to the
timetable of God, and that time was now up.

Small wonder, then, that in the opening chapters of the Infancy Narrative we find Luke almost gleefully repeating no less than on five
occasions that "the time is fulfilled". Unlike
Matthew on the same theme, it is not so much
that the Old Testament is being accomplished
as that the design of history is coming into
fruition, receiving its explanation. Time does
have a meaning. And this accomplishment with
its sense of joy can be traced throughout the
whole of the Gospel of Luke (as well as in his
Acts of the Apostles). The seventy-two disciples
came back from their mission "full of rejoicing"
(10.17,20); the assembled crowds "rejoiced over

the marvellous works he did" (13.17); there is
"rejoicing over one sinner who repents" (15.7)
and "merrymaking and rejoicing" over the return of the prodigal son (15.32). On the journey
into Jerusalem, at the Mount of Olives, the
whole company of the disciples "began rejoicing
and praising God for the miracles they had
seen" (19.37), and the Gospel ends on the same
note: the disciples "went back full of joy to Jerusalem" (24.52). But Luke adds the correlatives to
this joy; the disciples spent their time "continually in the Temple, praising and blessing God",
and if we turn over the pages of his Gospel we
shall find that it is characterized by prayer and
praise.

Besides the *Our Father*, Luke gives us other
worthy anthems, all praising God for his present
intervention in man's history which redeemed
his promise of old to the Jews: the *Benedictus*,
the *Magnificat*, the *Gloria in Excelsis*, the *Nunc
Dimittis*. These hymns of praise, all in the small
compass of the Infancy Narrative, tell their own
tale by their very juxtaposition: the birth of a
Saviour is the form that intervention of God has
so wondrously taken and for which due praise
must be rendered. The scenes of traditional
Jewish piety described around Zachary, Elizabeth, Mary, Simeon, Anna—which would have
an appeal to members of no matter what race—

are echoed by further incidents in the Gospel.
Only Luke will allow us to catch a glimpse of
Jesus in prayer at his baptism, before Peter's
acknowledgement that he was the Messiah, at
the Transfiguration, on the return of the disciples from their mission, on the Cross and with
the two disciples at Emmaus. We can clearly see
the importance of these incidents for the faith
and work of a Church so recently born. It comes
as no surprise to read in the Acts of the Apostles
of the early group of believers who "persevered
in prayer". The numerous other references to
prayer in the Third Gospel—the parables of the
Importunate Friend, the Unjust Judge, the
Pharisee and the Publican, the admonitions to
watch and pray, even to pray for persecutors—
show that praise is not the only reason for
prayer. The new age has brought with it responsibilities which can be honoured only with the
assistance of prayer. And Luke has not neglected
to give us an account of what those obligations
are.

Social and personal life

We are shown the Baptist telling the crowds,
the tax-collectors, the casual soldiers standing
by, the extent of their responsibilities. We find
in Luke a deep criticism of riches (echoing, perhaps, a crisis among the poor Jewish Christians

of Palestine). The Beatitudes stress the poor, the
hungry and the afflicted. Matthew may say,
"Blessed are the poor in spirit", but Luke insists
on the concrete reality: "Blessed are the poor."
Instead of Matthew's Magi, Luke gives us the
lowly shepherds. Poverty is underscored in the
price offered to "redeem" the infant Christ in
the Temple. We have also in Luke the parables
of Lazarus, the Wedding Feast (where the poor,
the crippled, the blind are guests of honour),
the parable of the Widow's Mite. The danger of
riches is exceptionally starkly painted by Christ's
words as found in Luke: "Woe upon you who
are rich . . . who are filled full" (6.24f.), and
"Keep yourselves clear of all covetousness"
(12.15); we cannot serve "God and Mammon"
(16.13). In fact, the majority of Christ's sayings
against riches are proper to Luke's Gospel and,
significantly, even those which are common to
all three Synoptists receive a more compelling
form in Luke.

Social responsibilities and an attack on the
dangerous power of riches—we can discover also
in Luke a more extensive asceticism than in his
fellow Evangelists. While the common tradition
will remind us how the pattern of Christ's suffering and resurrection must be re-enacted in
our own lives if we would be his followers (Matt.
16.21–3,24–6), Luke will go further and demand

detachment from all things. There must be no
reliance on possessions, but on God who will
provide; consequently, "Sell what you have and
give alms." (12.13–33.) To the conditions of
discipleship Luke adds that one must forsake
home, parents, brethren—even one's wife.
(18.29.) The full scope of detachment of mind
required is stated succinctly in 14.33: "None of
you can be my disciple if he does not take leave
of all that he possesses."

Luke, then, the Evangelist of the design of
God in history, imbued with all the joy of the
new age, is, at the same time, severely realistic
about the everyday demands of the Gospel and
will disallow any slackening of the high tension
involved in the counsels of perfection. History
has been redeemed, but there are demands of a
higher order. The grateful return to be made to
God for his intervention in Christ is that the
beneficiaries will carry their cross "daily".
(9.23.)

A universal community

The second facet of Luke's message we have
to examine is his universalism, his view of the
world-wide expansion that the Church must
claim as her due. There can be no doubt that
Luke was captivated by Paul's idea of a universal Church which derived from the teaching of

Christ. In his Gospel, Luke is at pains to under-
line those events and saying from Christ's life
which stress this essential element of Christianity. (In the Acts of the Apostles we see Luke
sketching that principle in application.) While
we search in vain for mention of the word
"Church" in Luke's Gospel, we cannot escape
the impression that a universal community is
being evoked by Christ. From an obscure, ex-
clusive corner of the Roman Empire comes a
religion forced by its own nature to create a
world-wide community. And while Matthew is
anxious to show that the rupture with the Jewish
people was something of a condition for the expansion of the Gospel, Luke prefers to see this
universalism as part of the design of God, part
of the plan of saving history.

It is permissible to try to disengage from
Luke's account the form this universalist teaching has taken. The story of the birth of Christ
is recounted in its appropriate setting. A group
of pious Jewish folk, living in hope of the fulfilment of God's promises in the Old Testament,
find that their expectation has been rewarded:
the Child born in their midst is greeted as their
awaited Messiah. Then, without warning, we
are transposed to a wider world-picture—the
Empire of Rome, signalled by the introduction
of the surrounding machinery of Roman rule:

"It was in the fifteenth year of the Emperor Tiberius' reign, when Pontius Pilate was Governor of Judaea, when Herod was prince in Galilee, his brother Philip in the Ituraean and Trachonitid region, and Lysanius in Abilina . . ." Luke is asking us to make the first attempt to see that what he is recounting has larger horizons than a quick glance might indicate. The whole world is implicated.

A similar care not to confine the Christian message to its Palestinian home ground can be detected when we compare, in the Gospel, Luke's treatment of matter which is common to the three Synoptists. He will avoid nearly all Hebrew or Aramaic words in his sources, replacing them with genuine Greek expressions; particular Jewish interests (especially legal ones), like Christ's controversies with the Scribes and the Pharisees, questions of observance, even the law of Moses as referred to in the Sermon on the Mount (Luke prefers "Plain"), are soft-pedalled. Yet anything of world interest is to the fore. This is not to say that Luke is anti-Jewish (an old criticism)—he simply wants to emphasize what is of importance to the Hellenistic world at large. Hence, on the positive side, to show the universal mission of Christ, he offers us such texts as "Peace on earth to men that are God's friends." In his genealogy, Luke does not con-

clude (as did Matthew) that list of Christ's
human forbears at Abraham, the father of the
Jewish race, but goes on back to Adam, the
common father of the human race.

During the public ministry, Jesus exhibits an
unheard-of regard for Samaritans, for whom the
Jews had a thoroughgoing contempt. Jesus seeks
hospitality in a Samaritan town (9.52ff.); ten
lepers cured include a Samaritan, significantly
recalled by Christ as the only one who returned
to give thanks; we have also the parable of the
Good Samaritan, with its fearful indictment of
the Jewish ruling classes which places in greater
relief the common humanity of a Samaritan out-
cast. Lastly, the risen Christ tells the Apostles
that repentance and the remission of sin should
be preached in his name to all nations (24.47)—
the echo of what Simeon prophesied in the very
Temple of Jerusalem itself: "This is the light
which shall give revelation to the Gentiles."
(2.32.)

The Temple

This mention of the temple of Jerusalem
brings us to an interesting query on Luke's
message. Despite his acknowledged universalism, how is it that such arresting signposts are
found pointing to the Temple in his Gospel?
It begins with a scene in the Temple in which

Zachary is involved; Jesus, in his earliest years, goes up twice to the Temple (2.22–38,41–50), both of which visits can claim a special symbolical value also; at the beginning of the ministry of Christ, the triple temptation ends, not as in Matthew at the top of a high mountain, but on the pinnacle of the Temple (4.9–12). In the most original part of Luke's Gospel of that ministry, the "Lucan Journey" of 9.5–18.14 (in which Luke, under the literary convention of a "Journey", has collected various aspects of Christ's teaching), we find that mention of any place which might distract attention from Jerusalem is omitted. Three times, on the other hand, is attention focussed on the city. And when Christ does enter the city with his disciples, his entry is "solemn", and he proceeds to the Temple. Finally, the Gospel ends where it began—in the Temple.

Now in this conjunction of Christ with the Temple, Luke has something more to offer his readers than just a reminder that, after all, salvation does come from the Jews; something more, too, than a recognition that the missionary activity after the Ascension started from Jerusalem. Luke, in this alignment he has made, has a deeper meaning; he wants to emphasize, even to a non-Jewish reader, the divinity that was Christ's. God was taking possession of his holy

Temple. And to one so close to Paul as Luke, the Temple was being replaced by that other temple of the divinity, the Body of Christ, the new dwelling-place of God with man, now no longer confined to Jerusalem. The way to the Temple was no cul-de-sac; this present, exalted Lord who was Christ transcends the confined Jewish worship and reaches out to the world. Because of this status of Christ salvation is made accessible to all. Within, once more, the Infancy Narrative, which does so much to place Christ for us, we find jostling with those references to the Temple an incipient Christian vocabulary of salvation (1.69,71,77), through a Saviour (1.47;2.11), by the saving power of God (2.30).

God and the individual

The third aspect of Luke's message that calls for comment is his way of presenting Christ. Besides acknowledgement of his divinity and of his role as Lord and Saviour, there is another facet of Christ which is intimately connected with these and which has, in Luke, an importance all its own. Jesus appears as intensely human, manifesting everywhere the benignity of God towards struggling humanity. The mystery hidden in Christ is accessible to all; for God there is no longer Jew nor Greek, nor slave nor freeman—all may approach him. The *mysterium tremendum* has become the *mysterium fascinans.*

Sinners find in Jesus a "friend" (7.34)—a fact witnessed to by the common Synoptic tradition, yet placed in great relief by Luke (as the episode of Zachaeus, 19.7, well illustrates). Sinners, on their conversion, become the privileged ones in the sight of God (15.1–32), the sphere of influence for the exercise of his longanimity (13.6–9, the parable of the fig-tree, so different in interpretation from Matt. 21.18–22). We are shown Christ pardoning those responsible for his death, pardoning the good thief—and even the crowds strike their breasts when leaving Calvary (23.48).

Then women, so inferior in Judaism, occupy in Luke a place of honour—Mary, Elizabeth, Anna, the Widow of Naim, the sinner whose name is so delicately omitted (7.36–50), the devoted women who followed Christ to the Cross (23.49,55;24.10f.), Martha and Mary. We may interestingly note the women, *dramatis personae,* of some of the parables (15.8–10, the woman who loses a silver piece, 18.1–8, the widow seeking redress). It has already been observed how those outcasts, the Samaritans, gained a place in the affections of Christ. In a word, while Mark has given us the mysterious Son of God, and Matthew the divine teacher, Luke has comple-

mented the picture by sketching in Christ as the
divine friend and saviour of man. Luke is always
seeking to describe Christ's personal contacts
with various types of individuals. Matthew may
set his scenarios on a mountain, away from the
haunts of men, but Luke is fond of the setting
at a dinner-table (5.29, Levi's; 10.38–42, Martha's and Mary's; 11.37, the Pharisee's—plus the
allusions to repasts in 5.39;14.12–15;15.1 . . .). His
Gospel presents us with an album of snaps taken
of various characters Christ has met. We can
spot entries that resemble a rogues' gallery and
pages that might have adorned a society illustrated. The differing reactions to Christ of such
sharply contrasted people, his various attitudes
towards them, are a lesson in themselves. And
everywhere is manifested the kindness of Christ.
A similar personal touch is noticeable even in
Luke's post-Resurrection narrative. Matthew
may give us an awe-inspiring incident on a
mountain, but Luke tells us of Christ joining
up with two perplexed travellers on the road to
Emmaus, of how he accepted their offer of hospitality, and of how (again, at a dinner-table)
he made himself known to them in the breaking
of the bread.

The reason for this trait of Luke's is not hard
to define. The collective sense of solidarity in
which the People of Israel had received and

transmitted revelation would be meaningless to those outside Jewry, among whom his Gospel was to be an instrument of salvation. An appreciation of the value of the individual, we have remarked earlier, was to be found among those of Greek culture, a humanist value. It is part of Luke's message that this sensitized point of contact will react to the dynamism of Christ, friend and consoler of humanity, but especially its loving Saviour. His breaking down of all barriers between races and individuals in a sympathy for all types and conditions of men—there we have the first signs inaugurating the universal community the Church was destined to become, with its hope for the individual.

Sacraments of the divine presence

Luke, then, that first Christian humanist, in his message of the New Age, the universal scope of the Christ-Event and the divine solicitude for the individual, has bequeathed to us a view of the world which receives God through a number of "sacraments" of the divine presence.

The first is the Temple, where one is at the religious centre of the world. But that Temple is now with us in a more resplendent and yet in a most human way. The community itself is also a "sacrament" of God who lives in it and makes it a place of spiritual expansion, in some way

his extension in time. God reveals himself in
history, too, involving himself in our fate, redeeming us through its saving events. The
"things that have been accomplished among us"
are like a patrimony on which we live; our
Christian history is always present to us. Finally,
in the Christian perspective, the individual,
even, is a "sacrament" of God's presence, because God is dealing not only with masses but
with men. The old pessimism, which surren-
dered God, and the new optimism, which
neglects him, both call for a corrective. God has
had the delightful courtesy to offer himself to
each man. Here we have the actuality of Luke,
and another writer has resumed it all for us—
"the philanthropy of God". (Titus 3.4.)

6

ST JOHN'S MESSAGE

A different approach

To take up the Gospel of St John after reading the Synoptists is rather like finding oneself
in outer space after having booked merely from
Paddington to Charing Cross. Not only are the
familiar sights and sounds of the bustling world
of the Synoptists just passing earth-echoes; the
whole atmosphere is rarefied with the strange-
ness of another planet. What happened when we
turned that page from Luke to John, that new
leaf which opened out into a new world? Behind
this query lies the involved series of problems
that enmesh the Fourth Gospel, questions about
the type of man that author was, his background
and the influence this exercised on his work;
questions about the way his homilies reproduce
the mind of Christ and about the quantity of
cold fact contained in his records; questions,
finally, about his actual work, its unity, its order,
its original composition. For a Gospel which has
more than its fair share of problems, we can
only hope to touch on those which have a direct
bearing on its message, and so in this attempt to

appraise John's offer of doctrine our principal aim will be to try to hear the themes of his symphony and avoid becoming too distracted by the technical problems the orchestra is mastering.

But before any investigation of John's message, there are certain specific traits which have to be examined which should serve as pathfinders to unearth—and unravel—his teaching. These will take the form of both recurring theological notions and the use of symbolism.

Any comparison of John and the Synoptists, besides showing how they differ on a number of chronological data (the calling of the Apostles, the cleansing of the Temple, the time spent in a Judean ministry, the date of the Last Supper) and in their presentation of Christ's teaching (John gives no parables, only extended discourses), illustrates an unusual contrast in the vocabulary of the Evangelists. To take some examples, we find that "love" occurs in John some forty-four times but only nine times in Matthew and six in Mark; "truth ("true") forty-six times in John, but only twice in Matthew and four times in Mark and Luke; Mark will give us "to know" on a dozen occasions, but John repeats it some fifty-seven times; "life" is recorded in John thirty-five times, but only seven times in Matthew; John has "light" in twenty-three instances, and Luke only in seven. These examples could be extended further ("Father", said of God, reaches the total of one hundred and eighteen references in John over Matthew's forty-five), but our business is with the theology which underlies this vocabulary of John.

The examples we have just cited hint that we shall be disappointed if we expect to find in the Fourth Gospel the terminology of the Schools— "Christology", "sacraments", "ecclesiology", and the like. What we shall meet with are notions which, if we may so put it, are more fundamental, much more profound. For purposes of convenience, we can divide these notions into two main groups—those which deal with Christ, the incarnate Word, and those which tell of the great gift of God he brought: eternal life.

The incarnate Word

In the Prologue of St John's Gospel (1.1–18) are to be found the taproots of the whole of his theology, that vast organic growth that was possible only since God became man. Neither properly an introduction nor a summary, those first eighteen verses contain the source of John's message. Paul may have his horizons filled with the exalted Christ of the Resurrection, Mark may be preoccupied with the mysterious Person who confronts men in the towns of Galilee and in the streets of Jerusalem, Matthew and Luke may even dare to whisper to us the secrets of his birth. But John will soar above these overwhelming mysteries to find his touchdown on the landing-place of eternity: "In the beginning was the Word; and the Word was with God, and the Word was God." The Word that was to make its first appearance at creation and continue this activity throughout the whole of Israel's history was (as the Wisdom literature began to suspect) not only with God, but God. And this Word, whose work had been witnessed to by a line of Israel's prophets, now came in person—"The Word was made flesh"—cast his tent among us, the new Presence among the new People of God. It is this union of the eternal and the historical, of the spiritual and the temporal, which gives significance to the whole of John's Gospel and which is (as we shall see) the reason underlying that symbolism characterizing John's records. But that is not all. Because the Word became Jesus Christ in time, a new world-picture is postulated in which eternal life is the only true life; into this he will incorporate us. No longer a question of the natural and the supernatural running side by side; in Christ they are united.

This incorporation of ourselves into eternal life, this new birth into divine sonship, is effected by the Word who is not only Son of God but also Son of Man. In him humanity is assumed, and it remains one of the major problems of our theology to uncover the riches of the biblical intuition on a doctrine of personality which associates the universal and the particular in one person. But, "to as many as received him, he gave the power to become the sons of God". Word, Son of God, Son of Man—how greatly the title of Messiah now transcends its Old-Testament parentage! Jewish ideas on the "unknown origin" of the Messiah receive another and deeper meaning with John; it was the Jewish belief that he was "to abide for ever"—but how differently from the high hopes held among a materialistic people; he was to be "king"—but John will show that his royalty is not of this world.

Behind all that John will say of Christ, of who he was, of what he did, is the governing and dominant reality, laid bare for us in the Prologue, that here was the eternal Word. This key concept explains the possibility even of such gifts as those which his coming offers to men and which John spends so much of his space in reviewing from every angle.

Eternal life

The principal benefit which Christ brought to men is, in John, eternal life. Other benefits which we can find in the pages of the New Testament—sins cancelled, the reception of the Spirit, the indwelling of Christ, union with the Father —are all consequent to that gift from above. The greatest thing the higher world had to offer was its form of life, eternal life. Although only realized in full after this present life has ended, yet eternal life is already present and actively lived. It is not still life. John tells us that such a life consists in knowing God, which for him is rather more than a purely intellectual apprehension; it is an experiencing of God's will in action through the person of Jesus Christ.

Hence it is that faith in Christ is essential to the possession of eternal life, particularly since he is no longer visible before men. Such faith makes possible that apprehension of the glory of God which Christ manifested to men, that revelation of God himself. John sees in this faith in Christ which opens the believer to knowledge of the Father and possession of eternal life, the ultimate reality, the truth *par excellence*. All else will pass away, but this, this is eternal. And this eternal truth is incarnate for us in Jesus Christ. It is not a matter of learning from him what the truth, the ultimate reality is; *he* is that, everything else secondary and diversionary.

Now through this faith in Christ, which John clearly sees as the mediating factor in man's

approach to God, is entered a personal and inti-
mate community of life with God that has the
character of "love", a union of wills. The
supreme act of love, Christ's self-immolation, besides its expression of God's love for men, carries
within itself a further significance: it insists that
love of God is to be carried into the streams of
history via the exigencies of everyday, practical
conduct. God showed his love in history; let man
do the same. Love of God, union with God,
mysticism in John's Gospel is controlled by the
taut clamps of daily existence.

The revelation of glory

Finally, John will have us aware of the basic
reason why God's activity from creation to the
Incarnation, his offer of eternal life and all that
this entails, were placed, as it were, at man's dis-
posal: to reveal to man his glory. It was through
the Word from all eternity that this glory of
God was mirrored; in time, the same Word, now
incarnate, manifested before men the same glory
of the Father. But it will be John's paradox that
the glory of the incarnate Word will be shown
at the time of his most abject humiliation, in the
moment of his death. Here, more than anywhere
else, was made available for all to see that light
which lit God's way to man and man's to God.

The darkness of sin was shown up in all its starkness and the light of glory confronted men with a choice: to share in the brightness of the light or to recede into the shadows it cast.

Christ's being raised up on the Cross was (in the Greek sense of the word) a *crisis*, a judgement. The darkness could not overwhelm the light of God's glory but it marked a discrimination: "This is the judgement, that the light has come into the world, and men have preferred darkness to light: for their works were evil; for everyone who does evil hates the light and does not come to the light lest his works be shown up as evil." (John 3.19f.)

Rejection of God's revealed glory in Christ, the light of the world, is described in John with all the profound pathos evoked by such a response to such a challenge of love.

Signs and sacraments

So much for a brief sketch of the theological notions which are the ingredients of John's Gospel. But there are also to be considered certain characteristic features which make an important contribution to its subtlety and depth.

We may note at the outset John's use of signs and symbolism. A simple event is recounted within the framework of everyday life, often with a slight humorous twist. This is followed by a lengthy discourse which sets out to measure that event in terms of eternal values. The event, concrete and historical, is no more than a "sign". But—and we cannot overestimate the importance of this observation—it is not a matter of separation between history and symbolism in the sense that a deeper meaning is placed at the side of, or imposed on, down-to-earth facts. It is the Johannine idea of history which is at work: history for John is both phenomenal and mystical. History does have an interior and spiritual dimension, and John wants to signal this out to us. Each of the seven signs recounted is explained, then, by one or two interpretative discourses, and in each episode there is a dominant theme which governs both the narrative of the event and the discourse interpreting it.

Now this unity of event and interpretation, basic to John's mind, which refuses to settle (as we have already remarked) for a purely abstract mysticism, implies that his intuitions of the deeper meanings of his accounts are being submitted continually to the control of history. But of history which knows the invasion of this world by Christ, the incarnate Word. At each turn of Christ's life John perceives the divine and the human at work and so can draw from such composite actions both a temporal and an eternal message.

Christ's earthly actions were signs, then—and these signs are prolonged in our sacraments. Hence it is that many interpreters have detected in John, not only a Johannine sacramentalism which sees in Christ's mysteries actions patent of a wider reality which is true beyond the limits of time and space, but even (polarized around the two sacraments of baptism and the Eucharist) the whole sacramental life of the Church. It is not without great interest that we find also in John, in the body of his Gospel, mention of important Jewish feasts in relation to Christ's ministry. Chapter 2 deals with the Passover in Jerusalem, Chapter 5 speaks of "a feast of the Jews" (possibly another Passover), Chapter 6 again the Passover, Chapter 7 the Feast of Tabernacles, Chapter 10 the Feast of Dedication and in Chapter 11 Christ's last Passover. Is it too much to see in these peculiar references of John to the Jewish feasts a suggestion that the old Temple liturgy was giving way before the present Christian dispensation with its climax in Christ's own Pasch?

Such, then, are the theological notions we find in John and his use of symbolism, which have marked the formation of this Gospel. We have now to see their employment in that Gospel.

The structure of John's Gospel

If we take time off to read the Fourth Gospel
in one sitting, we cannot fail to notice that it is
difficult to discern a well-organized plan in the
accounts before us. Many attempts have been
made (not only by Continental scholars who
have a flair for this sort of thing) to define
ordered divisions in John's matter, and many
"plans" have been proposed. But such attempts
are well proving otiose; John did not offer everything cut and dried, he did not mistake intricacy
for depth. Yet, if we cannot disengage, properly
speaking, a plan in John, what we can trace,
however, is an organic development of those
themes we have just been discussing. Professor
Dodd explains: "A theme is introduced and developed up to a point; then a second theme is
introduced and the two are interwoven; then a
third, and so on. A theme may be dropped, and
later resumed and differently combined, in all
manner of harmonious variation" (and we are
indebted to the same scholar for his work on the
argument and structure of John). Hence, we
must see in this Gospel, not a clear-cut enumera-
tion of ideas, but rather a thick texture of the
same—which, instead of being picked out in
isolation, are developed by means of each other,
one acting, as it were, as a precipitate on the

other, drawing out all its implications. Now we may perceive in this organic development a certain structure which is the result of that organic development rather than its cause. What, then, is this structure?

It is, briefly, that John presents eternal life (not salvation or justification, as in Paul, not the Kingdom of God, as in Matthew) as the outcome of the work of Christ and the main object of his message. And this message is evolved in such a way as to suggest the history of eternal life as God's gift, beginning with its birth in the soul and ending in a final victory of life over death. Incidents are recounted as various illustrations of this central theme according to an order which best serves to develop it. This is the body of John's message as found from Chapter 3 and to Chapter 11. In the Prologue we have been given the key to the whole situation: the Actor in the drama is the Logos, the incarnate Word. In the last part of the Gospel, the Passion account, we are shown the climax of all that went before, and earlier themes are restated to show how eternal life is to know God, to be both the subjects and the objects of his love, through which men are united to God and with each other.

In chapters 2 to 12 we find seven sets of incidents which treat of the work of the incarnate

Word among men. The first set (Chapters 2 to 4)—the marriage feast at Cana, the cleansing of the Temple, the meetings with Nicodemus and the Samaritan woman (between which last two, a second testimony of the Baptist is interposed) —have, as their dominant theme, the new beginning that Christ's coming into the world instituted. This inauguration of a new order is tied down to everyday life in Galilee, Jerusalem and Samaria, evidently with the avowed intention of bolstering up the claim of the Prologue that the Word became *flesh*. The water of the Old Dispensation is giving way to the joyful wine of the New; the Temple itself must surrender to that other tabernacle of the divinity, the body of Christ; Jacob's Well and the Temple, symbols now of the blessings and worship of the Old Testament, must recede before the flow of living water of the New. The die has been cast, the new order introduced. We see, in a second series of incidents (chapters 4 and 5) —the healing of the ruler's son and of the Bethesda paralytic—the initiation of men into that which is truly "life". These two narratives bear a symbolism which shows the life-giving function of the Word, echoing the perpetual activity of the Father. And (significantly) the Gentiles are not excluded.

The bread of life

Chapter 6 contains the third set of incidents, a complex "sign"—the feeding of the five thousand, the passage of Christ over the lake during a storm, the "bread of life" discourse. The Word, we have just noted, gives life; but John will add a precision: Through assimilation of him by faith and the Eucharist. In the long discourse which probes the significance of the feeding of the multitude, two complementary motifs may be observed, faith in Christ and the Eucharist. The substance of these two parts goes back to Christ, but the thought of the Master is delivered with interpretations which the Evangelist has thought necessary to add in view of the sacramental practice of the Church—in fact, the eucharistic liturgy. So where the first hearers of Christ would primarily learn of their coming to him by faith, John's reflection on Christ's words would show how personal acceptance of the Word attains its apogee in the acceptance of his redeeming death. Assimilation with the Word is directly achieved by the sacramental means of the Eucharist.

A second aspect of this complex "sign" of Chapter 6 is the progression by which the crowd is led from false or insufficient ideas about Christ's status as Messiah and his role to truer notions. Here is a new and greater Moses who gives something more than manna; he gives, rather he is, the Bread of Life. The whole discourse ends with the first of many siftings, many discriminations, we are to find in John. But it is in the next episode that this question of the acceptance or rejection of Christ holds central place.

Judgement ·

The watershed of the Fourth Gospel is situated in chapters 7 and 8, which tell of Christ's ascent to Jerusalem for the Feast of Tabernacles and his controversies with the Jews there (chapters in which we detect the echo of passages in the Synoptic Gospels dealing with Christ's conflict with the authorities and the consequent Passion predictions). Manifesting himself as Messiah to Jerusalem, Christ clearly shows that his claims transcend the brute materiality of the Jewish expectation. He shows himself as the source of living water first, but a transposition is noticeable in that this symbolism is veering towards another which will occupy two later chapters— he is the light of the world. And the presence of an important formula for John is being emphasized: the revelatory I AM of the Old Testament (so profoundly different from the chatty "It is myself" of the Knox text), to recall Christ's eternal being and unity with God. But the ground-bass of this passage is the manifestation and re-jection of the Word as life and light.

Though Christ insists that he came not to judge, judgement does follow, indeed, on the stand taken as regards his manifestation of him-self. John, with an irony characteristic of the whole Gospel, indicates how, when men are arraigning Christ for judgement, it is themselves that are being judged. Cryptic allusions to the Passion are only to be expected in these chap-ters, since the rejection of Christ will imply his death.

This judgement by the light is more fully de-veloped in the next set of incidents (chapters 9 and 10) around the healing of the man born blind. It is the Feast of the Dedication of the Temple. In the earlier discourses, Christ as "life" has been the prominent theme; now (after the transition of chapters 7 and 8) the dominant theme is Christ as "light": "I am the light of the world." The discourse attached to the giving of sight to the man born blind contrasts light against darkness, points to the triumph of light. We might note how the situating of this miracle at the Pool of Siloam juxtaposes the idea of "water" (and its symbolism) at the side of "light". An-other point is that "Siloam" means "sent", and its mention here can suggest that recourse to him who was truly sent from above results in that true vision which is the light of faith. In this context also a baptismal overtone cannot be dismissed.

And, once more, there is a crisis, a judgement. The interrogation of the sometime blind man is nothing less than a trial of Christ, but it is his judges again who are being judged. The following incident concludes with sentence of death on Christ.

Resurrection and life

In the raising to life of Lazarus (Chapter 11) the idea of resurrection is to the fore and this theme is developed by means of what at first sight appears to be a simple conversation between Martha, Mary and Christ. Here (as elsewhere) John shows how, through a certain *double-entendre* and even misunderstanding of his words by the sisters, Christ is able to proceed with his teaching; there are two levels of understanding involved—a physical resurrection and a spiritual one. The believer possesses eternal life now, and Christ's power of bestowing life, which is present and active, will also effect the resurrection, both physical and eternal, of the dead on the last day: "The hour *comes* and *now is* . . ." Further, we learn that Christ's own resurrection is consequent on his self-sacrifice.

The concluding set of incidents in John's history of the offer of eternal life to the soul is described in the last verses of Chapter 11 and in Chapter 12—the anointing of Christ at Bethany, his triumphal entry into Jerusalem and the discourse on the occasion of the questions of the Greeks. It is the last Passover of Christ's life. Where, earlier, we had been shown Christ turning towards death, here, with his anointing, it is his burial that is envisaged. And as the sequel, we may say, to that symbolic burial, we have the triumphal entry signifying Christ's universal kingship as conquering Lord of life and death. In the discourse to those Hellenistic Jews, present for the Passover, are emphasized a number of important issues.

Firstly, there is, in the description of Christ as the disintegrated seed which bears an extensive fruit, a note of universalism: he draws all men to himself. Then there is the climax to the theme of the glory of God. John had earlier shown (8.18) how any teacher seeking his own glory gives his own message, not that of him who sent him. But Christ seeks not his own but God's glory, and so he receives that glory which comes from God. (8.50–5.) A progression is observable in 11.4, where we see that Christ's glory not only comes from God but is linked to God's. Chapter 12 tells us that the hour has come for the Son of

Man to be glorified and that this glory is not only free from self-seeking, but even demands self-sacrifice. This act of self-oblation, while drawing all men to him, is, nevertheless (once more), an occasion of judgement for the world.

An epilogue closes Chapter 12 and John's treatment of the public ministry. He lingers over the record he has written, recalling the "signs" which have mediated the message of divine life and light, and man's rejection of this gift—as if in a final attempt to save men despite themselves.

Farewell

The latter part of the Gospel, the story of the Passion, falls into two main parts: the Farewell Discourses and the Passion Narrative.

Three cycles of discourses contain matter which we find paralleled in the Synoptic Gospels as having been given in private to the disciples. Further, many themes are reassumed from the previous part of the Gospel but with a heightened significance—the Father-Son relationship, their mutual indwelling, knowledge, vision, are now viewed in the perspective of Christ and his disciples. Where before "life" and "light" had pride of place, now it is "love" that is the key-word.

An impressive scene opens the account of the

Last Supper: the washing of the feet of the disciples by Christ himself. This new "sign" draws attention, not only to that profound humility of the Incarnation (so well pointed for us by Paul in his Epistle to the Philippians, 2.6–11), but also to a further sifting between Christ and man. The Jews, the world, have rejected the light and have been separated from the Apostles; now Judas will make known his rejection and he too will be sifted. Then follows the first set of discourses, the dialogue on Christ's departure and return. (13.31–14.31.) "Going" and "coming" have the force of formulas for Christ's death and resurrection, his *transitus*, his journey to the Father through his death. Moreover, Christ crucified must be the way by which his disciples also will arrive at the same Father. Union with their dead yet living Lord is their passport to eternal life. And their love for each other must reproduce the love of God for Christ.

A period is placed to this first cycle by Christ's "Rise, let us go hence." This phrase (a cause of consternation among commentators, since some sixty verses of discourse are still to follow) should be seen rather as a challenge to confront Satan; John is transposing to a higher level the attitude of Mark at the approach of the arrest-party. In both cases, there is a real departure, but for John it takes the form of an interior disposition.

Christ and his Church

The second cycle, the discourse on Christ and his Church (chapters 15 and 16) develops, by means of the allegory of the True Vine, the theme of God's love for man and of how that love results in the mutual indwelling of men with God. This is followed, by contrast, with the theme of the hatred of the world for the Church; persecution should be a welcome sign that the disciples are no longer of the world but united with Christ, who also was persecuted, And, once more, this hatred entails judgement, a judgement which is to be effected by the Paraclete, the advocate—but an advocate turned judge. His function has already begun. As the first cycle ended with a call to battle-array, this cycle is terminated by an announcement of victory: "I have conquered the world."

The Prayer of Christ (Chapter 17) constitutes the last cycle of discourses and resumes much of what was contained in the first part of the Gospel and in the preceding discourses. Christ's mission has been accomplished—he has revealed God's work and word, and the disciples have attained faith and knowledge. They too must continue the same mission despite (and even through) that suffering the hatred of the world will impose on them. It has brought Christ to the Cross. He prays that his disciples may be preserved in God's possession, kept from evil, sanctified in the truth and possess overwhelming joy; that they (and those who come after them) will share the same unity of divine life enjoyed by Father and Son. As a result, Christ will be continually manifested before men. Their reward will be the vision of God's glory and the experience of his love.

In all these Farewell Discourses, one may detect three important orientations. There is a social perspective—salvation is only in the Vine, the Body of Christ. The knowledge of God, union with him, eternal life, is expressed both in personal and social terms as "love", and as a love such as is shared between Father and Son. Lastly, these aspects of eternal life are made available to men through a fact of history, through assimilation of the death and resurrection of Christ.

The Passion

In the latter part of the Passion Narrative (Chapters 18 to 20), we have the account of the Passion itself and of some of the post-Resurrection appearances of Christ. But in contrast to the earlier part of the Gospel, where the procedure has been narrative followed by explanatory discourse, here narrative has pre-eminence

(Christ's arrest, his trial, crucifixion, death and burial, the discovery of the empty tomb and the appearances to the Apostles). But the Farewell Discourses (which really presuppose the Passion) have already supplied the interpretation of those facts.

In the arrest, trial and crucifixion of Christ we have once more a complex sign which is developed by means of the very details noted by John: Christ's surrender of himself in the garden, his comments upon the charge of kingship, the manner of his death with the flow of blood and water from his side. There is an allusion to the earlier "signs" of the Gospel and a final interweaving of them with this crucial event. The water and wine of Cana are recalled with the water and the blood; there is the Temple which is to be destroyed and raised up in the process of destruction; there is the life- and light-giving Word accomplishing his role through his death; the bread of life is now in truth the flesh of Christ given for the life of the world; we are reminded of the raising of Lazarus with Christ's victory of life over death; the previous burial anointing and the consequent symbolic victorious entry into Jerusalem tell us what to expect as Christ's physical death approaches.

Is not the Passion, then, the all-embracing "sign"?

And yet this sign on the grand scale differs from and is superior to all that have gone before in that, whereas the previous signs derive their permanent value only from that which they signified, this present event is something which not only happened in time but has eternal consequences. History can never be the same after it. Even the other signs are symbols of this event. They are true on the spiritual level only in so far as the Cross is true, true not only spiritually and eternally, but even in time and history.

We may leave John with one brief remark about the post-Resurrection accounts. Something of the "glory" we see in Matthew is lacking in John in the descriptions we read of Christ's appearances. But this is in view of John's teaching that it was in his death that Christ was glorified and exalted. In his self-oblation Christ reached his highest exaltation, his brightest glory. For it was the supreme expression of divine love.